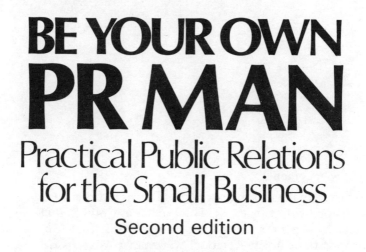

BE YOUR OWN PR MAN

Practical Public Relations for the Small Business

Second edition

Michael Bland

Kogan
Page

Acknowledgements

My sincere thanks to the people and organisations who
have helped with this book. They include: Colin Bell (Essex
County Newspapers Ltd); John Blundell (Institute for
Humane Studies); the Regional Newspaper Advertising
Bureau; Vic Francis (photographer); Stan Paice ('model');
Martyn Watkins (Ford Motor Company Limited), Mitze van
Rixtel, and Win, Helen Cudworth and Denise Philips for the
typing.

Illustrations by Derek Chambers

1037721 2

First published in Great Britain in 1981
by Kogan Page Ltd, 120 Pentonville Road,
London N1 9JN
Second edition 1987 (revision includes three
chapters from the same author's *Promoting
Yourself on Television and Radio*)
Reprinted 1990.

British Library Cataloguing in Publication Data
Bland, Michael
　Be your own PR man. - 2nd ed.
　1. Public relations
　I. Title
　659.2　　HM263

　ISBN 1-85091-417-6
　ISBN 1-85091-365-X Pbk

Printed and bound in Great Britain by
Billing & Sons Limited, Worcester

Contents

Author's Note

Public relations is probably the most sexually equal occupation of all. References to PR 'man', 'he' and 'him' in the text are solely for convenience and concise English. I dislike clumsy phraseology as much as I do discrimination.

The London telephone area code changes on 6 May 1990, and 01 will become either 071 (central area) or 081.

Introduction

This book is a disgrace. Just when the public relations 'profession' is establishing itself as a respectable institution, someone publishes a book which dares to suggest that sending a naked woman up in a hot air balloon is effective PR and can do your business a power of good.

But there's really no magic to PR. It does not require experts and it can be practised by any small business owner. It is something you can teach yourself. Indeed, as the person running the show you are better suited than anyone else to handle your firm's PR.

Public relations is the most neglected business tool. We devote untold time and effort to improving skills in finance, sales, personnel management, stock control, advertising and the many other subjects which together make for successful business. Yet for some reason the very term 'public relations' leaves many business people cold. Moreover, some of those who are aware of it are guilty of approaching it the wrong way, using PR to cover up faults rather than for establishing positive relations with their various 'publics'.

PR is as simple as you want to make it. It can improve business and boost sales for a minimum outlay. It can achieve results as good as, and often better than, normal advertising at a fraction of the cost.

Have a good look through the book and judge for yourself. After dealing with the question 'What is PR?' it deals with the general principles and shows in detail how to handle the press and broadcast media. Above all, it gives plenty of practical examples of how other people succeed.

It aims to take the mystique and baloney out of public relations and show you how it can help *your* business, sell *your* product or service, and give people a good impression of *you*.

Chapter 1
What is PR?

You're walking along the street and pass the offices of a big company. You're in a frivolous mood and the urge grabs you to pull a practical joke. You go through the rotating door and over to the lifts. You get out at the top floor, find the boardroom and occupy an empty seat just as the board is convening. You can sense them all peering over their bi-focals at you, moustaches bristling like so many antennae as they try to work out who you are. But no one wants to appear ignorant, so no one asks.

They waffle away for an hour or so about the company's plans and problems, and there is much coughing and spluttering about the new product which is about to be launched. Suddenly the chairman asks 'What do *you* think?' and you realise to your horror that he's looking at you. You've got to do some pretty fast bluffing and pretend to be one of their number, but if you pretend to be the finance director, manufacturing director, industrial relations director, planning director or company secretary they'll find you out in 30 seconds. So you pretend to be the PR director. By the time they catch on that you're not the real thing you're walking happily down the road again.

Laughable as it may seem, that episode could just conceivably happen because there are no set rules for public relations. The term means different things to different people. Ask 10 business people what they understand by 'finance' or 'sales' and you'll get 10 similar definitions. But ask them what 'public relations' means and you'll get 10 different answers. Some see it as cheap publicity, some as propaganda and some as a means of silencing the press.

Many practitioners see themselves as 'professionals'. Others regard PR men as buffoons and charlatans who serve no useful purpose in life.

No one even knows when public relations became an independent entity. People have used PR techniques, however subconsciously, from time immemorial, but its development into a specific business science probably took place in the 1920s in the United States (where else?). The first book on the subject, published in 1923, argued that the public relations professional had developed from the status of 'circus agent stunts' to 'an important position in the conduct of the world's affairs. People have been saying the same ever since.

PR is always supposed to be in this crucial stage of transition. Public relations people always tell you that they are in the process of becoming a profession and they will be saying it another 100 years hence. In fairness, many big companies take public relations very seriously. They are becoming more aware of their responsibilities to society and are starting to listen to their PR advisers, rather than using them as a mixture of publicists for good news and muzzles for bad news.

It's true that there are some skilled, experienced and scrupulous people in the PR business, but the science is too subjective and open-ended for anyone ever to define and codify it. Nonetheless, there have been many attempts. The Institute of Public Relations defines it as: 'the deliberate, planned and sustained effort to establish and maintain mutual understanding between an organisation and its publics'.

A more prosaic definition can be found in the advice of Ford Motor Company Limited to its dealers:

> It is fundamentally a compound of common sense, an undestanding of what the media really want, plus just a dash of flair. It isn't marketing, it isn't advertising, but it is complementary to both.
>
> The value of PR as an activity lies in its ability to increase public awareness of your business, and to put across your point of view — an increasingly important aspect of commercial life in these days of militant consumerism, environmental concern and public scrutiny of business affairs.

At the end of the day your definition of PR is what you want it to be. For one thing, who are the 'public'? Are they the press? Your customers? Your potential customers? Or are they the 'general population'? And what does 'relations' mean? Is it selling to them? Getting them to think highly of you? Conning them? Or is it simply grabbing their attention?

It's a bit of everything. In the last analysis, however grandiose your definition of PR, you are selling something — whether it's your product, yourself, your image or your views. If you fly a plane down the High Street with a half-naked model on the wing, it's a form of PR because you're making people aware of your existence. At the other end of the scale it's still PR if you pour millions into arts sponsorship for minimum publicity or chat up your MP without even mentioning the company's name.

A businessman's definition of PR will depend, too, on the size and scope of the business. Much of the public relations effort of the multinationals, for example, is devoted to improving the generally unfavourable opinion which people tend to have of anything big, especially if it produces smells, smoke or noise.

Many big companies spend millions of pounds on community programmes and charitable donations, some out of genuine altruism, some to keep the natives happy, and others a bit of both. 'Big PR' will often involve elaborate campaigns to change public opinion on one or more of its activities, for example the building of a power station or launching of a new drug. It is often used to try to change legislation in a company's favour.

Governments and authorities use massive PR campaigns to buy public understanding. Remember all the propaganda before, during and after the introduction of decimal coinage?

It can work the other way, too. Communities and pressure groups frequently use public relations techniques against companies and other organisations. Mary Whitehouse, Ralph Nader, the Campaign for Real Ale and CLEAR are but a few examples of people achieving tremendous publicity for very little outlay and no advertising costs.

Now let us just talk about PR for the purposes of this book. As a small business owner with limited resources you can rule out the sophisticated end of the PR business: corporate advertising, educational liaison and governmental affairs. For our purposes: *Public relations is about presenting yourself, your company and your product in a favourable light to your various 'publics' — suppliers, creditors, authorities, the general public and, above all, your customers and potential customers — at little or no cost.* It's about getting them to hear of you if they haven't heard of you before, and giving them a good impression of you.

Some of these objectives can be achieved by advertising. A cynical definition of the difference between advertising and PR is that advertising costs money. There's a big overlap, too, between PR and publicity. Again, the latter is likely to cost more and to be more blatant.

But the biggest difference is that something which is achieved by PR methods will usually be the most credible. For example, which do you find more believable when you're watching television: a commercial for a product or a documentary programme about it?

There's an old saying that if, at the end of a candlelit dinner, you tell a girl that you are fantastic in bed, that is advertising. If you tell her she desperately needs a man and you are the right one, it's marketing. But if at the end of the dinner *she* says that she's heard you're a great lover, and please can she go to bed with you, *that's* public relations!

One aspect of public relations is that, unlike advertising, publicity, sales and marketing, there is no 'bottom line'. If you put x pounds into an advertising campaign you can monitor the results and show a return of y pounds in extra sales. PR doesn't work like that, which is one reason why smaller businesses tend to shy away from it.

Another reason is that PR seems to have some mystique about it. If you don't know how something works, and can't see the benefits, it is understandable that it should be stuck on one side while you get on with something more immediate.

But just read through the book and look at the many real-life examples of how small business owners have used PR to their advantage. In doing so you should get a feel for the subject and form your own definition, which will be better than any number of written descriptions.

It's a reasonable question for anyone, especially a businessman, when faced with a new proposition, to ask 'What's in it for me?' Instead of several pages of waffle about the advantages of PR, let the examples in the book speak for themselves. Then you can make up your own mind. Just as appetisers, here are some brief case histories:

The landlord of a Henley pub dramatically dropped his drink prices for a period. It caught the public imagination. Not only did the local press cover it but it spread to the national press and he even had an interview with Jimmy Young on BBC Radio 2 in which he told a few million potential customers the name of the pub, what a great place it was and the name of the brewery which owned it. The idea has been used before and since in many different ways, a favourite one being to charge 'old prices' of some sort or another. The press love it, the drinking public love it and it brings in new customers.

*'the landlord of a Henley pub dramatically
dropped his drink prices for a period'*

Then for sheer cool you can't beat the boss of a micro-electronics company who landed some free publicity for a new mini-computer range by holding a press conference to expose how other companies in the business were ripping off their customers. Knocking the competition can be very dodgy and it isn't being recommended here as a PR method. But it's an example of how, with a bit of extra thought and a different 'angle', an otherwise ordinary piece of business can be turned into 'news'. Again, it made the national press and gave prominence to the company's name and products.

Every day business people are investing in new equipment, opening shops and factories, launching new products, taking on staff (or losing them), buying things and selling them. It is so humdrum that hardly any of it appears to be of public interest.

Yet in almost every one of these activities there is the potential for a wider audience. Often it requires no more than a few minutes' extra thought to convert an everyday act into news and thus to make the public aware of your existence. You might do everything else right, but that extra dash of PR flair can often be the ingredient which sets you on the road to success.

The owners of an Edinburgh record shop, who also managed a new rock group, were convinced that their performers had real talent. The record companies consistently rejected their work. The group's managers, convinced that the record companies didn't bother to listen to anything from small-timers, cooperated with a music trade paper to submit recordings of existing top stars under the new group's name. All were rejected and one big company even turned down one of its own stars! It was described by one of the record companies as a 'cheap publicity stunt' — said, no doubt, as they wiped the egg from their faces — but the point had been driven home. The Edinburgh men had nothing to lose as their stuff was getting nowhere anyway. So it didn't matter who they upset, and the national publicity from their campaign would have made some record companies think twice before reaching for the rejection slips.

'a piece of PR which smacked of pure genius'

Who knows, with enough practice you could even reach the heights of the building company who pulled off a piece of PR which smacked of pure genius. They offered a highly expensive luxury flat as the prize for the first player to score a hole-in-one in a particular major golf championship. Fortunately, someone did just that and the amazing value of the prize, plus the newsworthiness of a hole-in-one, got the builder's name all over the newspapers, on a score of national radio and TV newscasts and into the bar talk of every golf club in the land. An expensive piece of publicity? Not really. It's a tremendous coincidence that a leading bookmaker had taken a bet that week against a hole-in-one which resulted in his paying out an amount which happened to be the same as the price of the flat!

And PR goes beyond simply getting publicity for one-off events. A small percentage of astute businesspeople use public relations methods to make themselves an integral part of their local community. Often an average citizen, stopped in the street and asked to name a few local companies, may not even be sure what a particular firm does. Yet the name will spring instantly to mind if a particular firm has stamped itself on the public consciousness.

When it opens a new store the door is ceremonially opened by a well-known actor or soccer star. When threatened by a new proposed law, it writes to the local MP and sends a copy, plus press release, to the local papers. The managing director and his colleagues give regular talks to the Rotary Club, Round Table, Women's Institute, schools and clubs. One of the leading golf club prizes is the 'Bloggs Trophy', named after Bloggs's Stores.

The possibilities are endless. Many ideas are listed in this book but, once you get the feel of it, PR is whatever you want to make it. It's the difference between total anonymity and people knowing that you're there. It can make a customer, dealing with you for the first time, subconsciously believe that he's familiar with your product or service. It can make people feel that you are trustworthy and your goods are reliable when in reality they haven't tried them before.

In some cases it's the difference between success and failure, though that difference is more likely to be decided by other skills such as business acumen and financial timing, and by the luck of the draw. What PR can be, however, is the difference between 'plodding along' and 'taking off', and in terms of the time and money required it is the most cost-effective business tool you can have.

Chapter 2
The Groundrules

Like poker, PR has guidelines but the game is really what you want to make it. There are many ways to set about it and (again like poker) the winner is the one with the most flair, not the one who knows most about the rules.

The aim of this book is to give you a feel for what PR can do for your business, and advice on how to set about it. But the best way to master the art is to give it a try. One conference or publicity campaign is worth a dozen treatises on the theory of communications and principles of public relations.

However, you will be that much more successful if you devote at least a little time to some of the groundrules. The equivalent of many books and many years' experience are condensed into this one chapter to give some guidelines which are worth keeping at the back of your mind.

In the next chapter we'll start looking at some practical ideas for boosting your business with PR. But bear with it for a few more pages. There are several useful tips to be learnt from a brief study of the general principles.

The first step is to have an organised idea of what you are trying to achieve and how you are going to achieve it. The stages of PR can be summarised as:

Aim: Why am I doing it? What are my objectives?
Audience: Who am I trying to reach?
Message: What am I trying to tell them?
Communicating: How can I get the message over?
Evaluating: Did it work? What can I learn from success/failure?

Let us look at these points in more detail.

Aim

We do many things in life without asking ourselves why we are doing them. Most of us will rush, dripping, from the bath to answer a telephone without wondering why we didn't stay in the bath and let whoever it is ring back later. Some people even go up the north face of the Eiger and don't know why they did it.

Similarly, many businessmen and women, including often the most experienced practitioners of PR, will throw themselves into a frenzy of speech writing or organise a press conference without stopping to ask themselves 'Why am I doing this in the first place? What do I want to achieve?' Often the answer is nothing more than 'It seemed like a good idea', or 'Well, it's always been done this way'.

So put some purpose into public relations. If each act has an aim you are more likely to set about it in the right way and see the job through to completion. You may also save yourself some time, hard work, money and wasted effort.

Below we outline some of the possible aims when conducting a PR exercise.

Boost sales

For the small business owner this is probably the biggest benefit PR has to offer. You might, therefore, start out by saying 'I want to attract potential customers by making my company's name or my product known to them, or both.'

If you want them to know your name you might, for example, think in terms of sponsoring the local football team or paying the bus company to run a free service on 'Smith's bus'. If it is the product or service that you want to promote, however, you could find yourself organising a press conference to unveil it, or offering your service free to a local celebrity.

Increase/regain confidence

Throughout the book we will look at many examples of how PR can be used to promote your firm or product. But it helps to know from the outset that this is what you are trying to achieve.

For instance, a well-publicised offer ('half price for old age pensioners') is not the best kind of PR activity if what you're really trying to do is increase or regain confidence in your product or company. If sales of your light bulbs have been dropping because of rumours that they go phut after two hours, then a cheap promotion might only serve to reinforce fears that you are trying to rid yourself of them. If it's *confidence* you want, you'd be better off presenting a gross of them to the local hospital, and publicising the fact that the hospital relies on your light bulbs.

Establish identity

There can be many reasons for wanting to make yourself or your company known. The benefits range from customers automatically choosing your product to the bank manager thinking you are a reputable company when you come cap-in-hand for a loan.

Most PR activities help in some way to establish your identity, particularly the 'good citizen' ones, such as sponsoring an award for the best policeman. An admirable example of using public relations flair to create a good reputation overnight was the small company which adopted the name of a well-known fictitious company in a television series. There are certain legalities to cope with, and clearly not every small business can do it, but in this case it was a resounding success.

Get things changed

Public relations techniques are often used to change people's minds. Examples range from sophisticated, low-key pressure on an organisation (such as a submission to Parliament or a government department) to mass publicity exercises such as blocking the High Street with the cheap Russian lawnmowers which are ruining your business.

Other aims

These are just some of the reasons you might have for conducting a PR campaign or activity. There are many others. For example, you may need at some time to explode a myth to set the record straight. There may be a scare that your meat causes food poisoning or that your new office block will spoil the view of the church. As we will see during the book, public relations techniques can be used to show the favourable side of what you are doing.

Or you may wish to establish some kind of community presence. This might be because you want to stand for Parliament or get a knighthood, or it may simply be that you genuinely want to help people and be a good neighbour. Similarly, many firms go in for a certain amount of altruistic PR, by donating educational aids to the local school, for example. In providing, say, wall charts for the school or giving a careers talk you might be recruiting future staff or simply promoting the useful role of business in society . . . or maybe a bit of both.

Indeed, you may have more than one aim in mind. A company might use a particular PR campaign to attract customers, recruit school leavers, reassure the shareholders and increase the chairman's chances of being elected Mayor. The important thing is that you know *why* you are doing *what* you are doing.

That way you'll be much more effective. While much can be achieved by just coming up with bright ideas and turning them into publicity stunts, unless there is some sort of order to it you will go through life flying off in all directions and missing opportunities.

Audience

Having established what you want to achieve and why you are doing it that particular way, the next question is '*Who* am I trying to get at?'

Many public relations acts are seen by more than one 'audience'. Holding up the London to Bristol train to protest against the new motorway over your factory, may be seen on the television news by half the nation. It might be a very effective way of attracting public sympathy but it will not go down too well with the planning authorities that you are really trying to influence.

Sometimes you may only be trying to get at a small target group. If you have developed a new saddle which prevents riders from getting sore backsides it will be easier and cheaper, and just as effective, to get it covered in the equestrian magazines than to seek massive national publicity.

Here are just some of the audiences you might wish to aim at:

Potential customers: increase business.
Existing customers: increase business; stop sales falling.
Creditors and shareholders: reassure them; increase borrowing

potential; put them in an understanding mood when you reduce their dividend etc.

Government and authorities: change unfavourable measures; improve business environment.

Schools: get at future customers and employees; change educational mistrust of industry.

Opinion formers (eg top businesspeople, academics, union leaders, federation heads): influence them to improve climate for your business, product etc.

Employees: improve their understanding of you, and *vice versa*; make them all salesmen for the company.

'holding up the Bristol to London train'

There are many more audiences, and many more reasons for wanting to reach them. One very important aspect of communication is to know your audience. This is often overlooked, yet how can you hope to put the right message over if you don't know how they think or what they want?

So always ask yourself: 'I want them to know *me*; do I know *them*?' Instead of firing off an angry letter to a government department, try asking them in advance how you should set out a formal submission. If you want to be interviewed on a radio programme to promote your new deodorant among the disco-going under-20s, do you want to get on Radio 4 or Capital Radio?

A good tip is to read regularly what your audiences read. You

21

can learn a lot about different groups of people from reading the *Daily Telegraph*, *Woman*, *Choice*, *Beano*, the *Morning Star*, and so on. Put yourself in their shoes, then you can relate what you have to say to the things that interest, excite or worry them.

So, before you even start a PR exercise, you must ask yourself:

☐ What am I trying to achieve?
☐ Who am I aiming at?

The Message

The next stage is to ask 'What do I want to *say*?' It is another seemingly obvious question which even professional communicators often fail to ask themselves before leaping into action. If you have worked out the aims and assessed the audience, the message should be fairly easy to create because you know why you are saying it in the first place and who you are trying to say it to.

In the case of a product, the gist of the message may be quite simply: 'It's here', or 'It's better than anybody else's', or 'It's safe after all'. If conducting a campaign against the council because of threatened eviction, the message will be 'You've got it all wrong!', and there will probably be various subsidiary messages.

We'll look at how to work out and organise a message in the section on TV interviews. How much you say will depend, of course, on the medium you're using. In a television interview you may find you only have a minute in which to say everything. A press release might be anything from 100 to 500 or more words, while in a speech you could have an uninterrupted half-hour to get your points over.

However long you have to convey a message, and whatever method you use, there should still be one 'core' message and just a small number of main points. People can only take in so much at a time. Once half a dozen or so points have been made, most people have to start forgetting the earlier points in order to assimilate the new ones.

So, whether you are holding a press conference to announce an invention, being interviewed by the local radio station about the fraud allegations against you, writing a press release about your new service or sponsoring the swimming team, there is a message to get over. Otherwise there is no point in doing it.

'sponsoring the swimming team'

On the subject of messages, always stick to the truth. Public relations usually involves presenting only certain aspects of the truth. This is fair enough as you are out to show yourself in a favourable light. But never lie. It will catch up with you.

The British discovered in the Second World War that the most devastating propaganda was that which was based on truth. In the same way, public relations is only effective if there is a decent company, product or service there in the first place.

If, like many companies, organisations and governments, you try to use PR to cover up defects and detract the newshounds, you will only be digging your grave even deeper for the inevitable day when you fall into it.

Another key principle of communication is simplicity. Always remember that the majority of people on the receiving end of your message are not familiar with whatever it is you are trying to communicate.

Gobbledegook means failure to communicate; simplicity and brevity mean impact. For example: whichever version you use, the Lord's Prayer contains less than 70 words; there are 197 words in the Ten Commandments and the American Declaration of Independence has 300; the EEC directive on the import of caramel products contains 26,911 words. Of the four, which do you remember least?

Don't think that all the PR 'experts' are themselves that marvellous at simplifying things. A highly expensive report on a communications seminar claimed, for instance, that the seminar had concluded that the best of the various methods was the 'application of sociometric methods of analysis to communications relationships'. With the 'professionals' producing nonsense like that, your attempts at PR can be as good as anybody else's.

Even the most complicated subjects can, with some thought, be put over more simply. Look, for example, at the financial columns of the mass circulation dailies. The journalists who write these columns are highly skilled in explaining complex material in simple terms.

We would all communicate far better if we stopped trying to impress each other with our command of the English vocabulary, and instead pinned up a notice in front of every desk and typewriter stating the following facts: *Two million adults in Britain can't read. Only 40 per cent of the country understand what is meant by 'vulnerable', only 17 per cent know what a 'decade' is, 13 per cent understand 'chronological', 4 per cent 'autonomous', and, if you describe something as 'empirical', 99 per cent of the population will have no idea what you're talking about.*

Getting the Message Over

We've now asked ourselves: What am I trying to achieve? Who am I aiming at? What do I want to say? The last question before the message goes out is: How do I get it across?

This is the stage at which public relations experts talk about 'channels of communication'; in other words the methods and media used to get your message out of your head and inside the heads of your customers, creditors, employees or whoever it is you are communicating with.

There are many of these channels. When you meet someone at a party and talk to them about your product it's a type of PR communication, as it is when they bump into someone else and tell them what you said about your product. Whether you get an article about your company in the local paper or take a petition to the House of Commons, you are using different channels of communication.

The most obvious channels of communication are the press, radio and television. Soon we will go into these in detail, but the point to remember here is that there are many different audiences for different types of press and programme. There are thousands of different magazines, trade journals, local news-papers, national newspapers, and radio and television pro-grammes. Only very rarely will you want to go for all of them at once.

There are, moreover, different ways of communicating with these media in the first place. An article praising your service or product in a trade magazine, for example, might have been achieved by holding a press conference, writing a press release, having the relevant journalists visit your factory, taking one of them out for lunch, or quite simply making a telephone call.

As well as the media there are many other channels, such as speeches, lobbying the authorities, using trade and represent-ative organisations and so on.

An excellent guide to the various channels of communi-cation, and indeed to organising PR generally, is to be found in *Public Relations: A Practical Guide* by Colin Coulson-Thomas (Macdonald and Evans). It describes in some detail the frame-work which we are only just glimpsing in this chapter, and it uses several case studies as examples.

Checking the Results

Having put the message out, the last stage is to check that it has sunk in. It sounds obvious enough, but very few people do it. There is little point in devoting untold time, money and effort to communicating with the public if you are getting the wrong message over, or not getting through at all.

There are several ways of finding out whether your public relations efforts are working or not. Some large organisations conduct surveys, in which professional researchers take a sample of public opinion to see if a particular campaign is working, and to assess what needs to be done. These are very useful but will usually be too expensive to appeal very much to the small business owner.

In the absence of such resources you can always keep a finger on the pulse by conducting your own one-man surveys. You are always talking to people — in the shop or office, in the street, the pub, at parties and on the telephone. Without be-coming a crashing bore, see how many people have heard of whatever it is that you've just been promoting. Did they get the right impression?

If you and your family and staff act as amateur researchers in this fashion, you'll have a much better feel for how your PR is working and what more you should be doing.

Keep a file of press and broadcasting coverage, too. Did you get more coverage than last year, or less? Was it the right kind of coverage? What are the important aspects that are not getting covered? Get someone at home or the office to record any TV or radio interviews and analyse them for points scored and missed.

Another indicator can be any change in numbers of attitudes of customers. If the local paper has just written a highly favourable article about your business and the next day your turnover doubles, it's a fair indication that the message has struck home. At the same time, though, don't rely too much on such results, or lack of them. It can often be bitterly disappointing to find that a concerted public relations effort which results in plenty of good coverage only produces a trickle of interest. Yet the message may have sunk in more than you realise. Even if they don't bite the first time they have probably seen the bait. If nothing else, it may teach you that PR is a continuing process and not a one-off activity to be conducted in the heat of the moment and dropped if there are no immediate results.

How to Start

Those, then, are the general principles of PR. They are all to do with asking yourself:

☐ What am I trying to achieve?
☐ Who am I aiming at?
☐ What do I want to say?
☐ How do I get it across?
☐ Did it sink in?

Before we start to look at the techniques in detail, bear in mind that you don't have to do it all from scratch. It's an area rich in ideas for the trying. All the time other people and other companies are carrying out their own public relations and the results are there to be read in the papers, heard on the radio or seen on television.

Every time you see someone pull off a publicity stunt, obtain free coverage in the press, plug his products and catch the public eye, ask yourself: 'Would that one work for me?' Make a note of other people's ideas and try the best ones out for yourself.

Another useful source of help might be a PR consultant.

There are plenty of them, even in some quite small towns. Most are ex-journalists or public relations managers who have set up on their own to offer a range of services: PR advice, publicity, preparing press releases and providing useful contacts.

If there is more than one to choose from in your area, ask each of them how he or she would set about handling your particular problem, and get an idea of what it will cost. Are they prepared to name some satisfied clients? If so, how has that client's public image appealed to you? Standards vary enormously. Some are highly professional (and not necessarily more expensive) while many are still charlatans of the old gin-and-tonic brigade.

Understandably, most consultants are anxious to give you the full service and commit you to a contract. But try them out on a few limited jobs first, or go for a short, trial contract. Unless you are very successful or ambitious you probably only need an experienced PR person to hold your hand for a few months while you get the feel for doing your own PR.

To find who the consultants are in your own region, look in the *Yellow Pages* under 'public relations consultants' (just after 'public houses'!), or try the local chamber of commerce.

Three useful sources of information are;

The Institute of Public Relations
The Old Trading House
15 Northburgh Street
London EC1V 0PR
01-253 5151

Public Relations Consultants Association
Premier House
10 Greycoat Place
London SW1P 1SB
01-222 8866

The Public Relations Register
26 Market Place
London W1N 7AL
01-437 3357.

Contrary to what they will tell you, though, PR consultants are not essential to handling your own public relations. They can be a big help, and may stop you from committing a few errors, but there is no substitute for your own drive, initiative and basic low cunning. No one knows your business better than you.

So why not see how you make out? Look through the practical advice in the rest of this book and have a go yourself.

Chapter 3
The Press

Here is a newspaper story:

> Joe Smith Travel have appointed a Widcastle man to their new post of business travel consultant. The travel agents have extended their services to companies and Mr Herbert Packem, 57, of Shakespeare Road, has joined them to liaise with firms. Mr Packem said: 'Very often somebody goes to the counter in a travel agent's and there is no time for agents to listen to them and give them top-notch treatment.'

The names have been changed but otherwise that item is lifted word-for-word from a real newspaper. It's all there: the name of the firm, who to contact, the new service being offered and even a quick stab at the opposition. And it's all very credible because it's the newspaper that's saying it, not an advertisement.

But how did they get the story in the first place? Seemingly, Joe Smith was on the ball and turned his company's latest development into news. This provided the newspaper with 'copy', interested the readers and presumably gave Mr Smith more customers. And it may only have cost the price of a phone call or home-made press release.

The other thing Joe Smith did was to understand what makes newspapers tick. He knew which ones wanted which material and how to approach them.

In many ways PR begins with the press. With Joe Smith's basic knowledge, almost anyone can increase public awareness of his or her business. And it really isn't difficult. Let us take a look at how newspapers work and how you and they can benefit each other.

Every time a new method of communication is discovered — radio, then television, Prestel and so on — some bright spark predicts the end of newspapers. But newspapers are like rabbits and stinging nettles. The more you try to put them down, the more they thrive.

A newspaper is so versatile. If you want the sports results first, you can't switch on the *Nine O'clock News* at 9.25 and work backwards to the headlines. To listen to the news contained in a daily tabloid on the radio would take more than three hours, and you can't wrap your fish and chips in a Viewdata screen or spend the night on a park bench under a hi-fi set.

Nor can you roll a television set under your arm, open it up and browse through it on the train, do the crossword on your knee and tear out the page with your daughter's wedding in to send to Aunt Matilda in Minneapolis.

As an item of record the newspaper will be with us for a very long time. Although the more recent media often have more impact and are more compulsive, they all leave a gap which can only be filled by newspapers. Just as most radio and television journalists get their essential training working for newspapers, so the public relations man should cut his teeth on newsprint. And just as the Fleet Street reporter graduates from the local paper, so the best starting point is with your own 'local'.

There are three main press categories — local, trade and national. Each has vastly different requirements and it is a mistake to try to treat them all the same. Running each publication is an editor who in turn always has to remember the tastes of his particular readers. And it's only when you put yourself into the mind of a journal's readers that you can get into the right mind to contribute to that publication.

So using the press for public relations is like a marketing exercise in which the first task is to find the right target audience to aim at. Having selected the audience you then choose the right gun for the job. If you want to attract interest in your firm's new running shoes you put your PR effort into *Athletic Weekly*, *Runner's World*, and the sports page of the *Sunday Times*, not into *Home and Freezer Digest* or a magazine for the elderly and infirm. Similarly, you don't try to attract the interest of the middle-aged rose-growing fraternity with an article in the *Morning Star*.

This may sound painfully obvious, but much time and money is wasted on the 'shotgun' approach when more could have been achieved with less effort using a rifle. The first criterion, therefore, is to know your weapons. Only by studying the many publications in the market can you get a feel for which are most appropriate to your activities. One pleasant exercise in DIY public relations is to arrive half an hour early for a train, especially at one of the big stations, and browse through some of the numerous newspapers and magazines on the racks. It is free, entertaining and informative.

We have already mentioned the advantages of editorial coverage over straight advertising. We are talking about getting the newspaper to say it for you. This is more credible than a paid advertisement. It's also free. But never divorce the two concepts entirely. Advertising and editorial matter have a lot of overlap. For example, most special supplements pay for themselves with the space bought by businesses in the same field as the supplement, such as an eight-page 'special' on banking containing four pages of advertisements for banks and similar services.

Most companies advertise in some form or other, and the principles of selecting target audiences and the right publications are similar to those of public relations. But public relations is really about getting someone else to advertise on your behalf, whether it's the local barman telling a customer how attractive your receptionist is or a newspaper carrying a feature on your marvellous product.

We can start by breaking our selection of 'weapons' into three broad categories: local, trade and national.

Local Press

By far the biggest gun in the armoury is the local newspaper. No other publication or news medium comes near it for credibility, interest and the thoroughness with which the general public reads it.

A local paper can range from a daily giant read by hundreds of thousands to a small weekly covering only a few towns and villages. Its value lies in the fact that the readers identify very strongly with their local newspaper. Like a bigger version of the parish magazine or club newsletter, it is so much more interesting when you keep reading about people you know, seeing pictures of familiar places and following the darts team from the pub on the corner.

The statistics of local newspapers knock other media into a cocked hat and the facts speak for themselves. Local and regional newspapers are the nation's biggest medium, both in numbers and advertising. Sixty per cent of newspaper readers say that, if faced with a choice, they would retain their evening newspaper in preference to their national morning newspaper. A survey conducted among just 16 regional papers unearthed no less than 300,000 members of the papers' women's circles and clubs. The same survey showed that more than 36 per cent of people cited local newspaper adverts as the most useful to them, against only 15 per cent for television and 8 per cent for national newspapers.

Most areas are covered by both a regional paper and one or more local ones; for example, a resident of Colchester might read the *East Anglian Daily Times* at breakfast, the *Evening Gazette* over a drink after a busy day at the office and the *County Standard* on Friday or Saturday.

There are many reasons for their popularity. One of the biggest is the classified sections, in which you can find or sell anything from a baby bouncer to a six-berth cruiser. Then there are sections of news from around the villages, local sports reports, the latest on the new bypass scheme and the all-important news about what the borough council is doing to stop juggernauts.

As a general rule the big morning regional papers tend to cover a mixture of national news and the major items from around the whole region, such as murders, fatal car crashes, bankruptcies, rapes, fires and all the other cheering little snippets that put you in a good mood for the day.

Evening papers are usually more parochial, though they still have many urgent national items to cover. The delight of a good evening paper is that you can find yourself reading the autumn Budget details in one column and the results of the Little Dozeford harvest festival marrow contest in the next. Weekly papers, by contrast, contain almost exclusively local material.

The joy for the business person is that local papers are not only about councils, fetes and cricket matches. They are also very much about business. Your business. There is scarcely a single item of commercial news that isn't worth a mention as long as there is something newsworthy about it. Take the next copy of your local evening or weekly and go through it, counting the items about businesses, shops and trades in the area.

Taking one such paper at random, here are the business items I found: cottage industry plan for a village; off-licence granted to wine trader; new 'leisure centre' for a local toy manufacturer; lightning walk-out at factory; transfer of hotel licence for new owners; local insurance company has new scheme for legal costs; new manager appointed for store, and a four-page motoring supplement giving plenty of coverage to local garages. This was an evening paper on a day when it didn't even contain its regular business column!

'you can find yourself reading the autumn Budget details in one column and the results of the Little Dozeford harvest festival marrow contest in the next'

The weekly paper that Friday contained a further 15 items about local companies, including another of the sort of beneficial plug you can achieve with a little effort. It was a small but eye-catching piece which said:

Timely Delivery

Problems over timely delivery of cereal seed will disappear this autumn for some East Anglian arable farmers. The X merchanting company, which has a branch at Y, has guaranteed pre-season early delivery on a limited number of varieties.

Coming as it did beneath an article on the settlement of the pay dispute at the Town Hall which resulted in rate demands being sent out, that item was probably read by just about every inhabitant in the neighbourhood, including, of course, the farmers. It was little more than an advertisement for X Ltd, but it differed from an advertisement in two ways: it did not cost a penny, and it was much more credible because it was the newspaper and not the merchants who were telling you about the seeds.

Note, too, that all this business news is in addition to information on charities, pressure groups and other organisations who can benefit from good public relations. The great advantage of local newspapers in PR terms is that they will carry items which the nationals won't touch: items about *your* shop, *your* factory, *your* garden centre, *your* garage, *your* consultancy, *your* practically anything.

So, let us look at how to promote your own business in the local paper, not just once, but frequently and regularly so that the thousands of potential customers who read it are aware of you and know that you are good to do business with.

The first question is 'Do you really know your local paper?' OK, so you read it. Maybe you like it. But have you ever read it through analytically, asking yourself what makes it tick? Is it bright and jazzy or heavy and sober? Does it like a good scandal? Is it a 'campaigning' newspaper? And above all, does it carry plenty of news about your sort of business?

The need to know and understand the paper is all-important because once you start trying to get your own business into the paper — in the same way as that seed company — you will need to know the sort of story they are looking for. Achieving newspaper coverage is a marriage between what they want and what you want. If they want something you don't have, or if you have something they don't want, then you've got problems.

Having studied the style and requirements, it is worth looking at how a newspaper works, how it is staffed and produced. Remember first that a newspaper or newspaper group is a commercial enterprise. It is there, like your business, to make money and that money comes from the cover price and sales of advertising space, usually more from the latter than the former. Like other businesses, the newspaper is run by a board of directors with a chairman and managing director.

Then there is the kingpin — the editor. He or she is ultimately responsible for the style of the paper and every word that goes into it. The editor cannot supervise every item, so other senior journalists are responsible for the different sections. There is a news editor, diary editor, features editor, woman's page editor, and so on. They, in turn, have reporters and correspondents working for them who specialise in the different types of material.

There are also many other people behind the newsprint. There are photographers, lay-out specialists, copy takers, compositors and all the back-up staff of any business, such as secretaries, accountants and receptionists.

The *éminences grises* of any paper are the sub-editors — the experienced journalists who mould the raw material into the finished product. They will take a blue pencil to the copy of even the most talented 'hack' and knock it into a shape which will fit the style of the paper and the number of words needed to fill the space required. 'Subbing' is an integral part of newspaper life, but because the reader doesn't see it happening it goes unnoticed.

It is important to remember the role of the 'subs' in your dealings with newspapers. Their job is crucial to the success of any publication, but at the same time they have a capacity for damaging relations between a paper and the people who supply the news.

You can spend weeks cultivating a good relationship with a journalist, days preparing a good story for him, and hours being interviewed and ensuring that he has the facts right. When, a few days later, the story comes out in a form entirely different from that anticipated the immediate conclusion is that the reporter has murdered your story. But before you go after him with a shotgun, check first that the subs (when something goes wrong there are always more than one of them) haven't had to chop it in half to make space for another story. Or it may be that the sub concerned knew your story wasn't newsworthy enough to merit a place on the page so he had to find a different angle and move the copy round a bit.

Similarly, you may think that a story about you is going to appear but never does. It doesn't mean that the journalist never wrote it. What is more likely is that the sub had to 'spike' it (put the item on a spike for future inclusion, which then seldom happens) in order to make room for a more immediate story.

If you are going to receive favourable coverage regularly you must take the rough with the smooth and go along with the weird and wonderful ways of the editor's policy, compositors' errors and subs' occasional sadism. If you pay for an advertisement you can call the tune and insist on everything being as you want it, subject to the law and the code of advertising practice, but if they are doing the publicising for you it must be done their way.

All the more important, then, to learn the rules of the game. Having studied your local paper objectively and got to know something about the way it is staffed, the next job is to understand something about the way it is put together and printed. There is no need for an in-depth study of printing methods but it is worth knowing, for example, that if you want a full-page feature about your new shop in the Friday morning weekly you don't ring them up at 5.00 pm on Thursday and ask them to send someone round.

A lot has to happen between the reporter handing in his article and its appearance in the final version of the paper. After the sub has done his bit and indicated the spacing, size and type of print required, the copy is transferred into actual print, usually nowadays by a sort of computerised typewriter. Meanwhile the lay-out man is designing the shape and style of the page (another stage at which you might lose a paragraph or two). On his instructions a compositor pastes the print and headings into place and fits in the photographs.

In this, the most common printing method for local papers, the whole page is then photographed by a special camera and the negative is etched chemically on to a metal plate which in turn is transferred on to the drum of the printing press.

If this sounds like a gross oversimplification, it is. All the trades involved — journalism, lay-out, photography, printing — take years to learn and are very skilled. There are hundreds of different typefaces and methods of turning the rough copy into a page of newsprint. Go back through your newspaper again, this time looking at it in more detail. See, for example, how sometimes the headlines are white-on-black instead of the usual black-on-white. Sometimes grey tints are used, or reds, or blues. Very large headlines have to be enlarged by the camera first before they go on to the page, and somewhere along the line someone has to proof-read the whole thing.

We will now look at how to make contact with the newspaper. One way of getting off on the right foot is to show an understanding of their problems and limitations. Most journalists will be delighted to show you round and describe how the paper is written and produced. And be sure at an early stage to ask what their deadlines are. Nothing gladdens a newspaper man's heart more than early copy or plenty of advance notice for a story.

Newspapers are a fascinating study on their own. This is not the time and place to go into details about production and the many techniques, but if you want to bone up on the subject there is an excellent series of books published by Heinemann called *Editing and Design*. There are five books: *Newsman's English*, *Handling Newspaper Text*, *News Headlines*, *Pictures on a Page*, and *Newspaper Design*. They contain far more detail than you will need for everyday press relations but are the sort of books that are interesting to read anyway.

Enough of this background stuff. It is time to make contact. Do remember that the aim is not just to have press *contacts*, but to establish good press *relations*. Ideally, you are seeking to establish the same sort of relationship as you would with a good business colleague.

Remember, too, that your local paper almost certainly wants to get to know you. There is no need to approach it with fear or trepidation. Journalists at all levels, from the trainee to the Fleet Street editor, are always on the look-out for new contacts. An ace journalist would sacrifice his home, his wife and even his life before he would let anyone get their hands on his address book! So when you approach journalists for the first time it is worth bearing in mind that you are actually doing them a favour.

Another fact to your advantage is that you are doing your own PR and not paying someone else to do it for you. Journalists always prefer the organ grinder to the monkey. If you are running your own shop, business, agency or pressure group you will be much preferred by the press because you are the boss. When looking for stories, quotes, statements and opinions they will go to great lengths to get 'Mr Bert Basher, Chairman of the company, said . . .', rather than 'a spokesman said . . .'

If you are going to take the business of communication seriously, a good press directory is essential. You may be able to handle the local newspapers without one, but for the national and trade press, radio and TV, a directory will show you what papers, magazines and stations there are, what they specialise in, who to contact, and the address and telephone number.

There are quite a few directories, the leading ones being:

Benns Media Directory (UK)
Benns Business Information Services Ltd
PO Box 20
Sovereign Way
Tonbridge
Kent TN9 12Q
0732 770483

British Rate & Data
McLean Hunter House
Chalk Lane
Cockfosters Road
Barnet
Hertfordshire EN4 0BU
01-441 6644

Media Link
13-19 Curtain Road
London EC2A 3LT
01-377 2521

Pims Media Directory
Pims London plc
Pims House
4 St John's Place
London EC1M 4AH
01-250 0870

Willings Press Guide
Reed Information Services
Windsor Court
Grinstead House
East Grinstead
West Sussex RH19 1XE
0342 326972

There are several distribution and courier services which specialise in sending press material to selected media lists. Two of the better known ones are:

PNA
13-19 Curtain Road
London EC2A 3LT
01-377 2521

Pims
Address above

Now, before picking up the phone, who do you want to contact? Don't automatically go for the editor. As well as being very busy, he or she rarely writes the stories and you won't get any preferential treatment just because you know the editor. It's more likely that you want one or more of the specialists, such as the business editor, diary editor or features editor.

Again, study your local paper (or papers) for the types of section. However, be warned on one point: many newspapers use syndicated material bought from big national newspaper groups. This will often mean that the material written by 'our financial editor' or 'our motoring correspondent' has in fact come from London and the paper does not have a financial editor or motoring correspondent.

The section you want obviously depends on the business you are in and the type of information you want the paper to cover. If you have just designed a new skirt, you clearly want the women's page. If, however, seeing the skirt caused the Mayor to trip up the Town Hall steps because he wasn't looking where he was going, it is more likely to interest the diary, which is always hunting for amusing looks at local life. On the other hand the skirt may have been designed not to ride up when stepping out of a car and may therefore interest the motoring page. (And, if your skirt, worn by a leggy model, made the Mayor fall down the steps, thus causing the coach carrying the local football team to swerve, bounce off a lamp-post and set fire to the Town Hall, then you might try the women's page, diary, sports editor, news desk and business page!)

It's a case of horses for courses and you really shouldn't have too much trouble selecting your first point of contact. From there you can start to get to know the other useful people at the newspaper.

Let us say for argument's sake that you have been running your own small builder's yard for a few years in the town of Widcastle. Business has been good. Now you are planning to hire a couple more full-time labourers, buy the plot next door and invest in a new truck and two new cement mixers.

On its own there may not be much of a story for the local papers but isn't it time you got to know them anyway? There is no need to wait till you have a story; in fact, it is better to establish the relationship before the big day when you land the sub-contract for the town's bypass. You read the *Widcastle Courier* when it hits your doormat at 6.00 pm each evening, and at the weekend you flick through the *Widcastle Weekly*. The *Courier* has a regular half-page about local industry. The *Weekly* does not have its own industry section, but contains plenty of news in its pages about Widcastle's trades and businesses.

The next step is surprisingly simple. Pick up the phone, dial the *Courier* and ask for the editor of the industry column. Likewise for the news editor of the *Weekly*. Remember that these people have peak periods when they need a call from a small builder with no story like they need a hole in the head, so ring the *Courier* by mid-morning before things really hot up, or mid-afternoon after the paper has 'gone to bed'. And ring the weekly early or late in the week before or after the period of pressure.

You'll be put through to the person you've asked for or to someone who deputises for him. Either way, place yourself in his or her hands. Explain who you are, what you do, why you think you should get together, and suggest a meeting. Contrary to popular belief, there is no need to hire a Rolls and take him to Widcastle's only entry in the Egon Ronay guide. Nor is there any need after the fifth brandy to proffer a fistful of used notes. With a few stupid exceptions those days are gone. As Humbert Wolfe said:

> *You cannot hope*
> *to bribe or twist,*
> *thank God! the*
> *British journalist.*
>
> *But, seeing what*
> *the man will do*
> *unbribed, there's*
> *no occasion to.*

Many journalists rate the consumption of alcohol as top priority and few will turn down the offer of a quick pint or two . . . or ten. Watch it, though. It's in the corners of small bars off Fleet Street that scandals are unearthed, divorces disclosed, crimes confessed to and more state secrets divulged than the CIA and KGB could ever hope to gather. Unless you know and trust your journalist really well you should hear alarm bells as soon as you start, after a few stiff gins, to say: 'Keep this off the record, but . . .' For both your sakes keep everything on the record or don't say it. And don't kid yourself that boozy and expensive entertaining will get you any more coverage. It might bring your journalist friends back time after time with the enthusiasm of stray cats to an old lady who puts a saucer of tinned salmon out on the doorstep, but it won't earn you any favours.

The purpose of meeting your contacts — be it over lunch, at a pub after work or wherever — is to see how you can best help each other. What sort of material are they looking for? What things does your company do that are of interest to them? Do you have plenty of experience in your trade or profession so that they can contact you for advice or information when they need it?

Don't just exchange office phone numbers, swap home numbers too. Is there anyone else at the paper you should meet? And, likewise, might any of your contacts be useful to the paper?

Having made the initial contact you clearly don't want to keep ringing up 'just for a chat'. The next stage is to stick a toe in the water when you think you have something worth covering. It's surprising how many events in the life of the average business merit a few column inches in the local papers. The crucial question to ask yourself is: 'If I didn't know anything about my business and was reading the paper, would this item interest *me*?' There is an old adage that what is *worthy* isn't necessarily *news*worthy. At the same time, a remarkable number of everyday things can appeal to the newspaper reader. Again, look through your next issue making a mental note of the many news items which have emanated from trade and business.

Almost any new activity is interesting to someone. Let us look at one or two examples:

☐ A shop stocks up with an item which is new to the area — a tool, a piece of furniture, a new foodstuff. If it does something different, looks different or tastes different from anything seen in the locality before, then people will want to know about it. You've gone one stage beyond just selling things and are providing something new. This is news.

☐ There is a new appointment in your company. A new face in a senior position. The public will come into contact with him or her. So, what does he look like? Where is he from? What was he doing before? What's his experience for handling the new job?

☐ You or one of your employees has done something out of the ordinary, received an award, won a beauty contest, a Duke of Edinburgh's Award, the pools. Again, it can be of interest to a wider audience.

☐ Your local company has a connection with something of national interest. For example, a small computer peripheral workshop has a contract to supply a nuclear submarine project, you have been commissioned to design the jeans for a pop star, or your bookshop now has the first copies of that book which has caused a national scandal.

☐ Similarly, you are involved in something of local interest. Your building company is to build the new sports hall, the speedway team have taken out an insurance through your brokerage, or your toyshop is providing toys for the children's ward at the hospital.

☐ If you're game, let them know that you are prepared to comment on local and national issues. 'When asked how the one-way system would affect local shops, fishmonger Ron Skate said . . .', or 'The new prostitution bill will be ruinous for Widcastle's hotel trade, according to Joe Vice, proprietor of the Red Lamp Hotel.'

Just run your mind back through the events of the last year in your business. Couldn't at least one of them have earned a few lines in the local press? Could it be that you can actually help the papers by providing information about yourself and your company?

You can take things a bit further and look for the best ways to help them by providing material when they need it. For instance, when January 2nd falls on a weekday a morning paper has to be staffed and working on stories. But all the shops, offices and factories are closed. Apart from the usual idiot jumping in the sea, as he has for the last 60 years, it's notoriously hard to find anything to write about. So ask your contacts if they would like you to time that sponsored walk, long-service presentation or outburst against the council for New Year's Day. Some organisations even hold New Year's Day press conferences to give the journalists something to do.

The same principle can apply on a Sunday for a Monday morning newapaper. There are other periods which are very slack, notably the 'silly season' during the July and August holiday, when Parliament is in recess, many factories shut down and people go and bask on the beach instead of murdering one another and doing other things essential to the readers' enjoyment. Come up with a decent story in the silly season and you'll have a friend for life.

On a more day-to-day basis there is the news diary round which a newspaper revolves. If you give your contacts plenty of notice of dates when you'll be opening new premises, appointing a new manager or running off with your secretary, they can plan ahead and send a reporter and photographer and make a mental note of the space required.

Newspaper relations are a two-way business and can mean being forthcoming at bad times as well as good. Many people are guilty of swamping the newspapers with comments and press releases, then clamming up when there's an embarrassing story. A journalist will soon tire of the person who pesters him for coverage and then responds with a 'no comment' when it has been leaked out that the profits are down or a strike is brewing.

No matter how busy you are it's vital to give priority to calls from the press. Their deadlines are very tight. If you haven't got the figures in your head or you can't think of a suitable comment on the spot, say that you'll ring back in a few minutes. And do so. If they've hit a raw nerve and you really can't divulge something, promise the journalist that he will be the first to get the full story when it can be told, and try to stick to the promise. You can even tell him before you tell your employees so long as they are then informed before the newspaper is actually printed.

In fact, it is usually better to say you'll ring back after a few minutes than to respond off the top of your head. It gives you time to jot down your points and to make sure you don't make a complete hash of it.

Interviews

It is even more important to get your thoughts together and be certain of your facts and figures before a press interview. If a journalist is going to visit or phone you for an in-depth story, prepare a thorough brief for yourself in plenty of time. The principles of preparing a brief are described in Chapter 4, though the interview itself need not be such a tense, cut-and-thrust affair.

Unlike a TV or radio interview, you have the advantage of being able to expound more on the details and think before answering. Nonetheless it is as important as ever to think beforehand about just how you are going to express yourself on the important issues. Aim to get them to write about what you want to say, rather than what they want you to say.

As with TV and radio, never try to outsmart the interviewer. Half-truths, smart-alec asides and downright lies are a recipe for disaster. Be as open and honest as possible, but if you are sitting on any real secrets keep sitting on them. If he can't publish something what is the point of telling him? It's putting him in an unfair position to expect him to share your secrets. His duty is to his paper, not to you. The only exceptions are when the journalist is someone you really know and trust, and there is a genuine reason for telling him, or when you release a story with an embargo date on it (see the section on press releases).

Some journalists use a tape recorder during the interview. This helps with accuracy and avoids arguments afterwards. In some cases he or she will let you see the finished article before it goes to press so that you can check it for accuracy. In fact if you have any doubts after the interview it's a good idea to ask if you can see the final copy. The newspaper is under no legal obligation to show it to you — once you've said it there is no going back — but they will often cooperate if they can.

Once you have the copy in your hands, though, do fight the temptation to add afterthoughts or ask for bits to be cut out. You are only checking for accuracy, though they might be prepared to change the odd phrase if you think it is really important.

Press releases

The next stage in getting coverage is to do some of the work for them in the form of a press release. This is a ready written story which can save them the job of using a reporter to do the research, interviewing and writing. If you use a PR consultant this is the sort of job he could do for you as he should be able to write in the style that newspapers prefer.

If you write the story yourself (and there is no reason why you shouldn't) try to use the sort of language and style that the newspapers use. Think about it next time you read a paper. Here are some of the ways in which newspaper style may differ from the way you normally write things:

☐ Every item, no matter how short, should answer the questions: What? When? Where? Who? How? The question Why? can also be answered directly but should in any case come naturally out of the story.

☐ In general, articles are kept short and sharp. One of the great Fleet Street editors once said that there was no story which could not be told inside 40 words. Though that is an exaggeration it is worth remembering. Take this delightful example of a domestic holocaust which someone had to cram into a brief slot in the *Financial Times*:

> Court in Kirkcaldy heard Morris Kemp, 37, admit throwing a carving knife at his wife on Christmas Day before eating his family's duck by himself in the bathroom.

Admittedly it leaves you craving for more details of what happened on that fateful day, but you can't fault it for telling who did what to whom and when — all in the space of 29 words.

☐ The sentences and words are much shorter than you might use in, say, a business letter. The newspaper has to be understood by all or most of its readers and they are not all Oxbridge English 'Firsts'.

☐ There are usually no preambles. Most things we write — from the annual accounts to a 'Dear John' letter — require some sort of prelude to soften the reader up for what is coming, but the newspaper has to get straight into the story.

☐ They use direct quotes. It adds more colour and demonstrates that it is Mr Smith's opinion and not the paper's.

So how do you set about writing your own press release? Ideally, use A4 paper with your company's name and logo. Better still, if you are likely to send out press releases more than once in a blue moon, have some paper designed with your company's name and a bold heading saying 'Press information' or 'News from X Ltd'.

Second, of course, you must have something worth writing about. Newspapers are bombarded with unbelievable rubbish from all sorts of organisations. Representative bodies send out hysterical utterances on everything from abortion to the Budget, and manufacturers plug their products with the flimsiest of new 'pegs' on which to hang the story.

That said, there are all sorts of things which are worth putting into a press release and sending to the papers. Many of the stories about local companies in your paper stem from press releases put out by the companies themselves. The secret is to find what aspect of your own story is of interest to the readers. We discussed this earlier in looking for angles.

Supposing you are expanding into new premises or setting up a branch. 'Wholesale butchers Cleaver & Sons are to open a new freezer plant on the outskirts of town', for example. Big deal. All that means to the reader is that old man Cleaver has been exploiting his customers again and expanding on the profits. But that freezer plant is going to need people to run it, isn't it? So how about: 'Twenty more jobs will be created for Widcastle when Cleaver's new freezer plant opens in . . .'

Or you've finally found a nice little job to keep Higgins out of the way till the meddling old fool retires. Why not get some kudos out of it for the firm and send the local papers a press release about it? Higgins will be so delighted at seeing his picture in the paper that he might even miss the fact that he hasn't got a pay rise out of it. Again, don't stop short at 'Mr Fred Higgins has been made Chief Paperclip Clerk of the Daylight Robbery Co Ltd'. Surely there is something else of interest about the man, even if it's only 'Widcastle bowls star Fred Higgins is to take on new responsibilities at Daylight Robbery Ltd . . .'

If you are voicing an opinion to someone — a stinking letter to the council about their Sunday trading policy or a speech to the Women's Institute on lavatory chain manufacturing — a press release can widen the audience considerably. After all, you've spent hours penning a letter of literary brilliance equalled only by Dr Johnson's missive to the Earl of Chesterfield, or gallons of midnight oil have gone into your utterances to half a dozen old dears at the WI. So why not find an angle and use it to start a press release thus: 'Widcastle's Councillors have been accused of being a corrupt bunch of mealy-mouthed, cretinous half-wits by a local tradesman . . .', or 'Dumping of inferior Japanese lavatory chains could lead to the collapse of Widcastle's biggest industry, a local manufacturer warned the townswomen at . . .'

Here are the main ingredients of a press release:

Headline. The story should have some sort of heading to give the reader an idea of what it is about. Keep it short and don't waste too much time on it because no matter how good it is the subs will write one of their own. If they use yours it makes them feel insecure.

Beginning. Start with a bang. Imagine that you are writing it for someone who has just had supper and has a club committee meeting later in the evening. He's flicking through the paper while keeping half an eye on *Coronation Street* and is only taking in a sentence or two from each story to get the gist of the news.

The facts. Answer the questions What? When? Where? Who? How? Notice how many news stories answer these questions early in the story with devices like: 'Leading businessman Joe Soap has warned Widcastle that prices are out of control. Speaking to 200 members of the Order of Dead Skunks at the Skunk Hall last night . . .'

Quotes. Always try to add the human touch of somebody saying something. That promotion for Higgins, for example. He may not have put two words together in his 40 years with the firm but at the very least you can conclude with him saying: 'I'm delighted with the new appointment. It will give me more scope for making even bigger piles of paperclips.' On a more serious note, somebody else's quote can add credibility, such as 'satisfied housewife' Mrs Sproggs expressing her approval of your latest hairdressing technique.

Keep it short. Subs love 'fillers' for small blank corners, and they hate enormous chunks of copy which mean rearranging the whole page. Try to keep to a single side of A4. Only use more if it's a really important story.

Keep it simple. Here is an extract from a genuine press release: 'Slideably received in each bore for reciprocation therein is an annular piston pivotably connected by a piston pin to the upper end of a connecting rod. The lower end of each rod is rotatably connected to the conventional engine crankshaft by means of the usual bearing. The latter eccentrically mounts the connecting rods opposite the usual counter-weights . . .' No prizes for guessing how much coverage it got!

Layout. There are a few simple rules. Bear in mind that some harassed sub editor will be much happier if it's easy to see where it has come from, what it's about and who to get hold of for further information. And he will need space for alterations and printer's instructions. Here are the main points:

☐ Give your name, address, phone number and the name of who to contact.
☐ Don't forget the date.

☐ State whether it is for immediate release or for use later.

☐ Leave space at the top for printers' instructions to be written in by the subs.

☐ Use double spacing to allow room for alterations and leave plenty of space between paragraphs.

☐ Don't carry a sentence or paragraph over on to the next page. This can cause havoc with any subsequent 'cut and paste' work.

☐ If using more than one page, write 'more' at the bottom of each page. Number the pages and when you've finished write 'ends' to let them know you've finished.

Embargo. If the press release is not for immediate use then it is important to say when it can be used. The purpose of an embargo is to allow the press time to edit and place an item in advance. Take the annual accounts, for example. You know the figures already, so you can write the press release and issue it under embargo until the time of the official announcement, for instance: 'Embargoed until 11.00 am Thursday, 10 February, 19 . . .', that being the time of official publication of the accounts.

If the actual time of day isn't important, embargo it for '00.01, 10 February, 19 . . . ' or whatever date is appropriate. And remember that a lot of newspapers 'go to bed' early, particularly local weeklies which, though produced on a Friday, may be printed on Wednesday.

Or that speech to the WI. You may want to give the paper a chance to digest your wisdom and send out the speech in advance 'embargoed until time of delivery' (making sure that if the speech is cancelled for any reason you tell the papers). Repeat the embargo on every sheet in case they are separated.

There are all sorts of reasons for embargoing information. You may be announcing the result of secret negotiations, bringing in price increases on a certain date or announcing record profits. The press usually respect embargoes. While you cannot be entirely certain that your sensitive information is in completely safe hands between the time it arrives at their offices and when the official date is reached, it should be as safe as it is at your accountant's or printer's. Once in a blue moon someone from the media is hauled up for 'jumping' on embargo, but these cases usually concern front-page headline stuff, not your attack on Japanese lavatory chains.

By the same token, only put an embargo on something when there is a good reason to. You won't be thanked for slapping embargoes on items which could really go out at once.

Having prepared the press release, allow time for any typing and duplicating before it goes out. This is particularly applicable where large numbers of copies are required (eg a 'drop' to the national media). All too often a boss with a 5.00 pm deadline will tinker with the exact wording of a press statement until 4.30 and then expect it to get out in time after retyping, copying, collating, envelope stuffing and despatching.

If just a few newspapers are involved it will suffice to use carbon copies or photocopies. With larger numbers you may need to duplicate or use Multilith. If you don't have the facilities there are plenty of small copying agencies.

A last important point is to make sure that the press release reaches the right person at the right time. Avoid using the post if possible, and even then only mail a press release if it is embargoed for publication at a later date. The best bet is hand delivery, which is seldom a problem with local papers, though it may be more of a headache with the national press.

Mark it for someone's attention, preferably one of your contacts, such as the diary editor or motoring correspondent. It is a good idea to ring the intended recipient when you are about to despatch the release so that he or she can keep an eye out for it.

Remember the newspaper's deadlines and allow plenty of time for them to sub the press release and find a place for it, and again think about the timing. Most newspapers have busy and slack periods, so aim for the latter and get the release in a couple of days before the newspaper's publication date.

The finished press release is shown on page 50, and key points to consider are enumerated on page 51.

PRESS INFORMATION[1]

Daylight Robbery Ltd,[3]
Ripoff House, Usury St, Widcastle[4]

Contact: Jim Mean   21378 (Office)
                                  33631 (Home)[5]

For immediate release[6]

BOON FOR LEFT-HANDERS[7]

Widcastle's left-handed people will benefit[8] from a new product which goes on the market this Friday.[9] Called the 'leftimug', it is a useful mug with the handle on the left instead of the right.[10]

First to put the product to the test was left-handed pensioner Herbert Conn. 'It's a godsend', he said as he swigged cheerfully at his second mug of tea, 'my old mug had the handle on the right and I was always slopping tea down my shirt. Now I won't spill a drop.'[11]

The new mug will be on sale at Daylight Robbery's store in the High Street[12] where Daylight's Managing Director, Jim Mean, is offering a free tea bag with each mug for one week only.

ends[13]

30 February 19XX[14]

A sample press release

Notes

1. *'Press information'* or *'News from . . .'* identifies the document immediately at the newspaper office. That way it is treated as incoming copy and can't be confused with letters or advertising material.
2. A *logo* isn't mandatory but it's good PR to have some sort of 'house style'.
3. Tell them who you are with the *company's name*.
4. An *address* is essential.
5. The *name* and home and office *telephone numbers* of the person for the newspaper to contact if there are any queries or if they want to develop the story further must also be included.
6. A *release date* (ie embargo) early on tells the news-paper which issue the item should go in. In this case, as you're not putting the mugs on sale until Friday you could release the story earlier in the week under a Friday embargo (if there's no specific time it's a useful idea to mark it for 00.01 Friday, 30 February 19XX). But, if there's no imperative reason for specifying a release date, don't clutter the subs with unnecessary requirements. Mark it 'immediate', bang it in to their offices at the beginning of the week and let them find a place for it. This one is a pretty thin story and will stand a better chance of being published if you are as cooperative as possible.
7. The *heading* is short, simple and to the point.
8. The story says early on that the reader is learning about something which will benefit local people.
9. The question 'When?' is answered early on.
10. The question 'What?' is also broached quickly.
11. Next comes the human touch. This one gets in a direct *quote* about the product and is also a plug from somebody local.
12. Having captured the reader's interest in the mug, he or she will want to know 'Where?'.
13. 'Ends' or 'more' tells the sub whether you've finished or if there is more to come on the next page.
14. The *date* is important for your records and theirs, and particularly for the odd press release which gets lost and turns up on the desk a couple of weeks later.

Press Release Checklist

- ☐ Date.
- ☐ Preferably on headed paper.
- ☐ Head it 'Press information', 'News from . . .' or similar.
- ☐ Give an address, phone number and name of contact.
- ☐ Say *when* it can be used ('immediate' or 'embargoed until . . .')
- ☐ A short, simple, relevant headline.
- ☐ Answer: Who? What? When? Where? Why? How?
- ☐ Look for a human touch, and a local one if it is for the local press.
- ☐ Don't carry a paragraph on to another page.
- ☐ 'More . . .' at the end of each page, and 'ends' at the end.
- ☐ Use direct quotes where possible.
- ☐ Leave plenty of space — at the top, in the margins, and between lines and paragraphs.
- ☐ Keep the whole thing concise and punchy, with simple language and short sentences.
- ☐ Accompany it with good photographs.
- ☐ Make sure it gets there!

Photographs

In a newspaper a good picture really is worth a thousand words. No amount of lurid description of, say, an air crash can tell as much as a photograph of the smouldering wreckage. Nothing can beat an all-action goal-mouth picture, or a portrait of someone you are trying to describe. The press release about the leftimug is a good example of a story that needs a picture.

As well as telling a story or describing something, a photograph can add that all-important human interest to the columns of newsprint, especially in local papers where the good citizens can see something of the mayor, the police chief, the rat catcher and Miss Widcastle.

A good *balance* of pictures is important for the look of the newspaper itself. Too many, and it looks like a naughty magazine. Too few, and the paper can look like a nineteenth-century copy of *The Times*.

Newspaper editors like pictures, and many press releases can be enhanced by including one. Eight inches by six is a good size. It can be smaller if necessary, but don't make it bigger as many newspapers can't cope easily with large ones on their plate-making equipment.

Only use black and white (except for the rare occasions when a colour magazine or supplement is involved). While black and white prints can be made from colour film they lose a lot of their definition and quality. Clear prints with low grain and plenty of sharpness and contrast are needed for mass reproduction, especially for the newspapers still using letterpress printing which breaks the photograph down into small dots. The standard needs to be very high, not only because of the reproduction requirements but also because your picture will be competing with dozens of others for space. And by all means send more than one picture, as long as each is of satisfactory quality, and let them choose the one they like best.

Be very critical of a picture. Is it relevant to the subject? Could it tell the story 'on its own' with just a caption? Look at the subject and pretend you're a reader seeing the picture for the first time. Ask yourself 'So what?'

Most subjects can be improved by the inclusion of people. That leftimug is going to look very lonely and impersonal all on its own, so show it in use with the pensioner clasping it in his left hand and smiling happily at the camera. Instead of a boring shot of your new showroom, offices or factory floor, include some of the people who work for you to show that you employ human beings.

Once there are people in the picture get them to do something. If your photograph of the office includes a couple of executives and a secretary, it will look hopelessly dull if they are just sitting there smiling at the camera. Have one of the executives answering the phone while the other explains a document to the secretary. And instead of an ordinary portrait of your newly promoted manager (not that portraits are wrong) try a picture of him doing something, for example getting out of his car on his first day in the new job, talking to a satisfied customer or leaving the building on his way to a service call.

Look critically at the pictures in your own paper. Note, for instance, the lifeless pictures where a waxwork dummy of a boss hands over a gold watch to an equally immobile retiree while a row of employees look on like so many tulips.

Is some idea of scale required? Your pet shop has taken delivery of a rare Andalusian miniature camel. It is only two feet tall, but alone in a photograph it will look like an ordinary camel. So stand the wretched creature beside your labradors to give an idea of its real size. Or if the feature of your dealership's new estate car is its big capacity, get the local netball team to pile into it with all their gear plus nets and stands.

The Birth of a Product Photograph

1. The obvious thing is to send a picture of the left-handed mug with the leftimug press release. This is already a big improvement on words alone. The potential buyer can see the product instead of just reading about it. But on its own it looks pretty lifeless.

2. To show how different it is from the ordinary right-handed mugs you could show the two together for comparison. Be sure that the caption says which is which whenever there is more than one item.

3. Many run-of-the-mill photographers, their creativity deadened by years of asking the bride's mother to step back a bit to get her face in the shadow, will simply take a shot of the mug (dare I say a 'mug shot'?) and leave it at that. But the product has much more appeal if we see someone using it.

4. Having got this far, see if more impact can be achieved by 'cropping' the picture to remove extraneous material and close in on the mug, hands and face. Don't rely on the newspaper cropping for you. They are trained to do it but often fail to do so.

Photos: Vic Francis

5. Now we are getting somewhere. With a little extra thought, the subject wears a sling to give some real point to the left-handed mug. And note the satisfied smile that the photographer has squeezed out of him. It really does look as though the old boy has been gasping for a nice hot cuppa for weeks and has found salvation at last. Even then you could improve still further with some more cropping and more attention to detail (for example, he's wearing a watch on his left wrist, which gives away the fact that he's really a right-handed man posing for the job).

Take the case of the leftimug. There are several ways to photograph it. It could be standing on its own, or full of steaming tea. Or if your representative customer is clutching it, you might see a lot of him and a little of the mug, or a lot of the mug and a little of him. He could be looking lovingly at the mug or grinning gleefully at the reader. When the print is finished, take another look to see if it can be 'cropped' by cutting out some of the peripheral material to emphasise the subject. (Look at the range of product photographs on pages 74 and 75.)

Lastly, attach a caption to the back so that the newspaper can identify it, ideally with a typed caption (so that you can still get something in as a caption story if space is short). Use adhesive tape rather than gum, as gum crinkles the photograph when it dries.

All this advice is for you to know what you are looking for in a photograph, not to help you take it yourself. Some people do succeed with photographs taken by themselves or by gifted amateurs, but they must be very good indeed. Photography is one area of public relations where DIY is not recommended.

There are many professional sources. If you deal with a PR consultant ask his advice about photographers, or ring the photographers in *Yellow Pages* and ask if they do this sort of work. The National Union of Journalists (Acorn House, 314 Gray's Inn Road, London WC1X 8DP) has a directory of freelance news photographers in each region.

Don't overlook the available product pictures which most manufacturers use for their own PR. If you are looking for local publicity for something you sell, the manufacturer will probably be pleased to provide some pictures free. Also, the newspaper itself may be prepared to send a photographer for you. Ask your contact at the paper and give plenty of notice.

Whoever you use, don't be afraid to brief them with your requirements. Very few photographers, however brilliant they may be technically, are all that good at composing news photographs. The requirement is for a certain flair and imagination over and above the ability to get the light and focus right.

It is well worth reading *Pictures on a Page* by Harold Evans (Heinemann), a fascinating and absorbing study of news photography. Again, it contains more information than anyone but an editor or professional photographer will ever need, but it is eminently readable and well illustrated. Once you have browsed through it you will look at press photographs with a new eye.

Press packs

For some events it is worth considering a press 'kit' or 'pack'. This is a press release and photograph(s) plus other relevant material packaged together. A typical press pack might consist of a simple piece of coated cardboard which folds down the middle and has two half-pockets.

On the front cover you would have your company name and logo, 'Press information', and perhaps something like 'Announcing the new leftimug.' In one of the inside pockets you would have the press release and some more detailed back-up information such as a description of how the mug was invented and how it is made. In the other pocket would be a selection of photographs for the press.

Press packs are a bit lavish for the run-of-the-mill stuff like speeches and visits by celebrities, but they add a professional touch — for not too much extra cost and effort — to a product launch, the opening of a new store or some other big occasion.

Press conferences

For the really big events you may want to hold a press conference. This is when the press are invited to turn out *en masse* to listen to your pearls of wisdom. A press conference has its value when you need to talk to a number of pressmen at the same time, when, for example, you announce record profits and want to talk to more than one correspondent from more than one outfit. Or you may wish them to talk to more than one of your team or look at a product for themselves. A good strong 'peg' of some sort is essential. Journalists hate nothing more than turning out in large numbers only to find that there is no real story.

Select the journalists carefully and only invite those to whom the press conference will be directly relevant. At the same time, be sure not to miss any important ones. Are there any magazines which might cover your story? Is it worth a shot at the local radio station? Or TV?

Talk to your own contact, or simply ring the relevant desk at one of the newspapers, well in advance, to ascertain that your date is suitable. It is no use spending a fortune on a press conference to announce the leftimug if that is the day that Miss UK is in town.

Give plenty of notice and send out written invitations. They can be formal if you like but the best is a one-page letter of invitation which describes, in a low-key way, what the press conference is about and why you believe it is of use to them. Try to send the invitations to named individuals, or at least to the business editor, motoring correspondent etc. And if there is any human interest or potentially amusing angle, don't forget to send one to the diary editor.

Now for the organisation. It need not be a massive operation, but it is important to get it right. Years of hard work can go down the drain if the Widcastle press turn up at the wrong time or place, or if they rush out to phone their stories to their desks and find that there is no telephone.

The first thing to arrange is the venue. This can be either at a local hotel, hired rooms or on your own premises where you will feel more comfortable and the bill will be cheaper. The place does not have to be exotic or expensive. Journalists are more impressed by efficiency and pithy talk than by Louis Quinze decor. Before deciding on the venue check it out for:

☐ Adequate seating
☐ Privacy
☐ Acoustics and background distractions
☐ Facilities for visual aids if used
☐ Catering
☐ Cloakroom facilities
☐ Car parking and accessibility by other transport
☐ Nearby telephones
☐ And if radio or television are invited, ensure that there is a quiet room for interviews, with at least one 13 amp power point and preferably a high ceiling and a light-coloured decor for TV lighting.

Having established the place, date and time, send out the invitations, ideally with a simple map and an indication of where to park.

You are arranging a press conference because you have something to present or say, so it is important early on to organise how you are going to say it. As well as preparing a brief to deal with the questions (see Chapter 4), you will need some sort of introductory talk to set the scene, not the Gettysburgh Address but three or four minutes explaining your product, your stand or your cause.

The text of this introduction then becomes a press release which is handed out to the journalists — either on its own or in a press pack — as a back-up to the press conference. (By the way, hand out the press packs as the newsmen are leaving, not when they arrive. Otherwise you'll find yourself talking above the rustle of paper as they read through the press material and pre-empt everything you were going to say.)

Stick to very simple catering. Mid-morning is a perfectly good time to hold a press conference, with coffee when they arrive and, optionally, some drinks and nuts etc at about 12.00. Some press conferences involve a slap-up lunch. By all means feed and booze them if you want but it won't get you a single line of extra coverage. For the actual 'conference' arrange them in seats facing you and your team who are at a table. Make sure they can see you, using a platform or lectern if necessary. And make sure they can hear, but avoid using a microphone unless it is essential.

Involve your own partners and staff in the press conference, with senior people helping with the questions and answers and others chatting up and organising. Give them lapel badges saying who they are and what they do, and brief them beforehand not to try any clever stuff or talk off the record. Their best advice is to borrow a leaf from Robert Townsend's book (*Up the Organisation*) and be as open as they like with the press but at the same time to pretend that they are talking to someone from your closest rivals. That way they will be relaxed and friendly but not blow any secrets.

While not essential, it is an idea to hire a photographer. Occasionally a newspaper likes a photograph of 'Mr Smith announcing his exorbitant profits at a news conference today', and if nothing else the pictures are a record of the occasion. Have the pictures printed immediately afterwards and send them by hand to the people who were invited.

If announcing or unveiling a new product, have it on display if at all possible, with any supporting literature. And if using visual aids, such as film, slides, an overhead projector or a blackboard, have a dry run beforehand to make sure everything works.

A signing-in book is useful, too. Brief a tactful member of staff to ask them to sign in as they arrive. This can be very helpful for future use, such as following up with some new aspect of the story, providing future contacts and inviting the right people to future functions. An ordinary visitors' book, exercise book or even loose sheets of paper will suffice. The only details you require are as shown on page 80.

The big day arrives, a typical 'programme' might be:

> ### DAYLIGHT ROBBERY LTD
> *Press conference to announce leftimug*
>
> Seedy Hotel, Widcastle,
> 30 February 19XX
>
>   Name   Publication/programme

09.30	Someone checks venue for seating, catering etc.
10.15	Staff assemble, put on name tags and are briefed.
10.45	Stand by to receive journalists, who have been invited for 11.00. As they arrive they are greeted, asked to sign the book, introduced to you, and given a cup of coffee. You introduce the rest of the team.
11.00–11.05	Most journalists have arrived. Take your places at the table facing them and invite them to be seated. Leave someone on duty to greet latecomers and show them to a seat.
By 11.10	Welcome them. Brief explanation of purpose of press conference, describe arrangements for drinks, telephones etc, and explain that a full press pack will be handed out afterwards. Also explain facilities for TV and radio interviews if appropriate.
11.10–11.20	Introduction. Explain why the press conference is being held (describe product, its background, its use and future plans, announce profits etc).
11.20 onwards	Questions and answers. Floor open for press to ask any questions they like. In answering, follow the principles described in Chapter 4 but, as with press interviews generally, you can answer at greater length and in more depth (but never waffle). Whereas on the air you are trying to get a few points over in a short time with maximum impact to an unreceptive audience, with the press both sides can be more relaxed and analytical. Nevertheless, the old rules apply: say what you want to say, not what they want you to say, and remember that nothing is ever off the record.

Once the meeting has wound up, press packs should be handed out, drinks offered and the discussion continued informally.

Of course, a press conference can follow various formats and the length may vary from a few minutes to several hours depending on the importance of your material. Some are based on a lunch at which the proceedings really start when the company chairman dings an empty brandy glass with a spoon. This is the cue for him to make his spiel to rows of glassy eyes amid the dulcet snoring of those members of the press for whom the emotion of the occasion has been overwhelming.

As a rule aim for about an hour in total of professional presentation and questioning with no frills or gimmicks. The pressmen will respect you all the more for it.

As soon as the press conference is over, get the signing-in book and compare it with the invitations list to see who didn't come. Then send a messenger round with copies of the press pack for the non-attendants. The material in the press pack should already indicate whether it is embargoed or for immediate use.

Finally, do not be surprised by anything that happens at a press conference. You might organise one on the shallowest grounds, only to find the place packed with pressmen looking for some bizarre angle because they have nothing better to do that day. Or you can spend weeks preparing the most earth shattering material and find yourself holding forth to a trainee from the sports page. Don't be offended. It is nothing personal. In sending out the invitations and press kits you have, at least, reminded them of your existence, and even if only a handful turn up you can get to know them that much better.

Press Conference Checklist

- ☐ Arrange a suitable date and time.
- ☐ Send invitations in good time.
- ☐ Check venue for:
    - — adequate seating
    - — privacy
    - — acoustics
    - — visual aids
    - — catering
    - — cloakrooms
    - — car parking

— telephone

— radio and TV interview facilities.

☐ Brief your staff and rehearse.

☐ Signing-in book.

☐ Product on display.

☐ Introductory speech.

☐ Anticipate questions and answers.

☐ Distribute press packs after the event, and send to those who didn't come.

Supplements

Newspapers frequently publish supplements. They can range from one page in the *Widcastle Courier* on local restaurants to 20 pages in the *Financial Times* on finance for small businesses.

These have a dual purpose: they provide a service to people interested in restaurants and establishing a business, and they attract advertisers. The supplements editor or features editor aims to make a profit on the survey with sales of advertising space, and for many newspapers it is a highly profitable part of the business: hence the sometimes esoteric and pointless supplements which appear in otherwise responsible papers. These, however, tend to be the province of the up-market 'nationals'. The local newspapers are more concerned with practical subjects like housing and motoring. Try asking your contacts to tip you off if the local paper is going to do a supplement on a subject relevant to your business.

Better still, why not put the idea into their heads for them? It is surprising how many subjects can make interesting supplements — children's clothes, indoor plants, DIY, car maintenance, insurance, hotels and restaurants, sports goods, local artists, and so on. Since you know more about your business than they do, you can help by providing a list of subjects to be covered by the supplement and by acting as expert adviser on the material. It is worth a try, and if they agree to carry the supplement it should be possible to get a favourable mention for your company.

Be warned, though. It is the job of the advertisement sales department to persuade relevant businesses to buy space in supplements, and they can be very persuasive. Since you are getting some free coverage there will be some moral pressure to put something in the collection box.

There is no simple answer as to whether to advertise or not.

It's like the vicar asking you to run a stall at the church fete. It seems churlish to refuse though you don't really fancy it. Most people tend to go along with the newspaper and buy an advert, but it is not likely to influence the editorial material very much. Sometimes the sales people may imply that failure to cough up could result in no coverage for the business. This is nonsense, but relations may become rather strained if you take with one hand and don't give with the other.

Whatever happens, if you do advertise make sure that they separate your advertisement from the editorial material about your business. Newspaper readers may put up with all sorts of drivel but they are not complete fools, and nothing looks more contrived than an article about the usefulness of tea trolleys perched over a quarter-page ad for your company's tea trolleys.

Other local newspapers

Widcastle's *Courier* and *Weekly* are not the only types of local newspaper. There are others worth considering.

FREESHEETS
Nobody knows how many 'freesheets' there are. These are the newspapers which are stuck through your letter box whether you like it or not and the delivery boys always cut across your rose bed to the neighbour's house when you're not looking. They have grown at a phenomenal rate in recent years and are still growing.

Most areas have at least one freesheet. Typically, it is put together by a devoted handful of people in a third-floor office consisting of two rooms and a gas ring. They are financed by sales of advertising space at lower rates than other newspapers, and remain profitable because of their low overheads.

So put two and two together and you can see that editorial material is not their strong point. They have to rely on any scraps they can scavenge, so almost anything you send in will be welcomed with open arms. The phone number should be in the freesheet somewhere, or in the telephone directory.

Get to know the local freesheet editor and you can be of real mutual help. As with local newspapers, though, be prepared to advertise from time to time to show willing.

Watch for new developments, too. Freesheets are becoming big business and some of the major regional newspaper groups are moving in to produce more professional rivals to the existing 'locals'.

LOCAL MAGAZINES

Most regions have their own glossy magazines based on happenings in the county or large town. You can find these in any of the newspaper directories, such as Benns; or ask at a large newsagent's. For the most part they are full of photographs of hunts, May balls, licensed victuallers' dinners, ladies' nights, golf club sherry evenings and Fiona Snottingham-Clatworth's coming-of-age party. They are financed partly by advertising and partly by bulk sales to the golf club and the Snottingham-Clatworths; hence the remarkable number of photographs, with captions, of otherwise unnewsworthy people.

Many of these magazines cover the local business scene and, like freesheets, need all the help they can get with material. It's a good way of getting news about your company read by the wealthier sections of society.

Your own newspaper

Quite a few firms publish their own occasional newsletter or 'newspaper'. These are more than just an advertising handout. They can carry news about developments in the company, latest products and prices, appointments, any awards or prizes that have been won, news about clients and people in the company.

These homespun newspapers can be distributed free to all sorts of outside audiences — suppliers, authorities, clients and potential clients. The advantage with potential customers is that it has the look and feel of a newspaper, so it is more readable than an ordinary advertisement or brochure. But probably the biggest advantage is with existing clients. It shows that you have remembered them and gives the clientele an exclusive, club-like atmosphere. It also reminds them of your existence in case they had forgotten.

Some firms publish a news*letter* which by its nature contains less direct product advertising than a news*paper*. Either form does the job, with the letter going more for the 'club' atmosphere and the paper for attracting new customers.

Both are fairly simple to produce. You will need help and advice on lay-out from a design consultant, of which most towns have several. A newsletter can be printed by a copying agency while for a newspaper you will need to go to a proper newspaper printing house. Even then you may be pleasantly surprised at the cost. For example, a four-page tabloid newspaper with photographs, a 'masthead' and one colour in addition to the black and white print would cost, at 1987 prices, around £350 for the first thousand. Larger numbers work out much cheaper: 5000 copies would be only just over £500. The run-on cost would be about £90 per thousand.

Distributing to clients and suppliers will be very cheap because it can be mailed out with the bills and payments. If you want to distribute to a wider audience it will start to cost more, but most freesheets have a reasonably priced distribution service and can do the job for you.

Summary

We have emphasised the central role of the local press: it is the most accessible, most precise and most widely read medium for your PR efforts. We have looked at a gamut of PR techniques — press releases, press kits, handling interviews and press conferences — and the whole question of building a relationship with the press in the context of *local* media. There are two other important and effective types of press: trade and national, and most of the principles we have examined in looking at the local press still apply. There are, however, one or two points to bear in mind when dealing with these other media, which we must now consider.

Trade Press

The remarkable thing about trade publications is that there are so many of them. It is small wonder that the tree is an endangered species when you consider how many of them must be chopped down to provide one week's worth of trade press. (Get a copy of the advertising pundits' magazine *Campaign* and you'll see what I mean.) They include the *Fish Friers' Review*, *Hairdressers' Journal International*, *Horticultural Abstracts*, *Industrial Lubrication and Tribology*, five different magazines for undertakers, 10 for fancy goods buyers and thousands of others.

In addition to all these magazines and newspapers there are trade newsletters. These are, in effect, trade publications which provide 'inside' information on the particular business you are in. Often the subscriptions are high, while the newsletters themselves are produced cheaply and require no pictures and few staff. The biggest overhead is the Rolls Royce.

'the remarkable thing about trade publications is that there are so many of them'

All these publications, from the glossiest magazine to the simplest newsletter, need material. Indeed, with generally low staffing levels they are avid users of press releases, articles and any other old junk you can throw their way. The sole requirement is that the material is relevant to the particular industry which the magazine covers and, preferably, that it is fairly new stuff. If it is well written, so much the better.

Before the editors of trade magazines start sticking sub-editors' spikes in my effigy let me explain that their publications perform a valuable function and are extremely interesting to their readers. They may take themselves rather too seriously and are full of 'in' jokes and references, but then they are not intended for general consumption.

So don't forget the trade press when publicising something. If, say, fruit farming is your line it will be of interest to the *Fruit Trades Journal* when you discover a new strain of extra juicy apple. But much more important is to think of other trade magazines which might use your information and bring in some customers at the same time. For example, your press pack on the new juicy apple should without fail find its way to the offices of *The Grocer*.

Most of these magazines are listed, with addresses and telephone numbers, in the major press directories.

Professional magazines might understandably be offended at being bracketed with the 'trade' press, but do not ignore them. Some are lavishly produced and have impressive circulations. They, too, are always on the look-out for material of interest to their discerning readers.

If yours is the first firm to import an electronic pen which can take dictation, write in four languages and tell you the times of the trains from Bristol to Paddington, you should not only contact *The Times* and the *Widcastle Courier*. What about the *Director*, *Management Today*, *Professional Administration*, *Chief Executive*, *International Management* and a host of others? They are all listed in the press directories.

National Press

Most of the principles for dealing with the national press are the same as for the locals but the nature of the beast is different in many ways. For most small businesses there is a lot more mileage to be gained from putting your resources and effort into the local press, where readership (in the area) and credibility are higher and there is less competition for space.

If 50,000 people read the *Widcastle Courier*, an item in it about your company will be seen by all 50,000. But a piece in *The Times* will be lucky to be seen by 5000 in the Widcastle region. To get through to all the *Courier* readers via the nationals, your story will have to appear in *The Times*, *Daily Telegraph*, *Guardian*, *Financial Times*, *Independent*, *Today*, *Mail*, *Express*, *Sun*, *Mirror*, *Star* and *Morning Star*, and to achieve that you will either have to murder somebody or remove a great deal of clothing.

So if your sphere of activity is within a certain geographical area it is not worth getting too excited about the national press. However, it's a different story if you want to attract a nation-wide audience. If you need to attract customers and others beyond the banks of the River Wid, time should be devoted to Fleet Street.

The first thing to remember is that the tastes and requirements of the national papers are so very different. Buy one morning's batch of newspapers and look at the different things which are presented in different ways to different people. There is no reason why you should not go for blanket coverage but

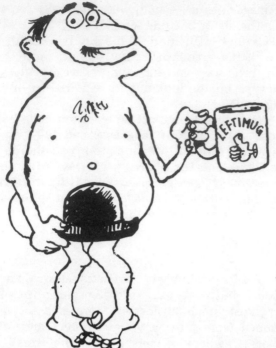

*'you will either
have to murder
someone or remove
a great deal
of clothing'*

your national press efforts will be more effective if you are aware of the different audiences. As one wit put it:

The Times is read by the people who run the country.

The *Guardian* is read by the people who think they run the country.

The *Financial Times* is read by the people who own the country.

The *Mail* is read by the wives of the people who own the country.

The *Express* is read by the people who want the country to be run the way it was 40 years ago.

The *Telegraph* is read by the people who think it still *is* run the way it was 40 years ago.

The *Mirror* is read by the people who want the country to be run by somebody else.

The *Morning Star* is read by the people who want the country to be run by another country.

And the *Sun* and the *Star* are read by people who don't care who runs the country so long as she's got big tits.

On a rather more sophisticated level, the best guide to what sort of people read which newspaper is to look at the job advertisements. The management consultants who place the ads have spent years working out who reads what. Get to know the job columns and you are getting to know your audience.

The Sunday papers are a still different animal. As there are fewer of them, each covers a broader spectrum but, once again, the job ads will tell you all you want to know about the readers. They are also notoriously hard for the run-of-the-mill PR item to get into. Look at the sort of things they write about and you will see why. But it is always worth a bash at the Sundays because every so often the up-market ones will go into depth and you can find your complaint about the dumping of Japanese lavatory chains making half a page in the *Sunday Times*.

Another paper with a difference is the *Financial Times*. Each issue carries a terrific amount of news about what is happening in the business world. The readership is small in relation to other papers but it is read by a lot of people with financial clout.

We have looked at trade magazines but there are, of course, hundreds of other national magazines which should be borne in mind. That skirt which doesn't ride up, for example, could grab the women's magazines with their enormous readerships.

There are business magazines, DIY magazines, photographic magazines and a whole army of others. If you try to cover them all with each press release the postage costs will bankrupt you, so it is only worth selecting relevant ones for each campaign. They are listed in categories in most directories, and you can always browse through the shelves at a large newsagent's to see which ones will suit you.

One major difference between the national and local press is that the former, understandably, will not be overwhelmed with enthusiasm if every small businessman in the country rings up out of the blue 'just to make the contact'. There is still no reason why you shouldn't get in touch and suggest a meeting to discuss whatever it is you're promoting, but only do so when you have something pretty solid to offer. And the national journalists (except for those on specialist magazines) have little time for blatant product plugs.

Finding the right contact is fairly straightforward as correspondents are usually 'bylined'. Each paper has a team of specialists for each area: finance, industry, consumer affairs etc. (One leading journalist, when asked what his new post as consumer affairs correspondent meant, replied: 'I consume things, have affairs and co-respond.')

Once you've got something worth talking about, be brave. Go on, pick up the phone and ask. There is nothing to lose even if you get the odd brush-off. The best time to call is late morning: any earlier and they won't be in, and by lunchtime the place is hotting up for the evening deadline.

For the Sunday papers, Tuesday and Wednesday are the best days. Most Sunday journalists have Monday off, and by Thursday things are starting to hum. Magazines prefer their copy well in advance.

Incidentally, the newspapers may aim at different social strata but the people who write them are pretty classless. The fact that a journalist writes short, simple material in the *Sun* or *Mirror* doesn't mean that he has to be taken for lunch to a whelk stall in East Ham. He or she is just as likely to have a first-class degree in Economics as a counterpart at *The Times*.

As with the local press, by all means take your contact for a good meal, but don't expect any favours. He will be just as impressed with you if it's a simple meal or a drink after work.

Having cultivated a contact, even the experienced PR people often waste the effort by not following up a story personally. In other words they send out press releases to the mailing list and hope that the journalists concerned will spot that the story has come from good old Harry who was so lavish at the Connaught Grill. If possible ring the best contacts to alert them that a press release is on the way. Give plenty of notice. That way they can set aside some time to work on it, and if they are away they can alert someone else to look out for it.

Even if you are located in or near London the actual delivery is more of a headache than with simply one or two local papers in one town. The old Fleet Street newspapers are in some far-flung places these days: *The Times, Sun, News of the World,* and *Sunday Times* in Wapping, for example, and the IPC magazines produced in 'no-man's-land', south of the Thames. And if your offices are outside London, deliveries to national newspapers can be an even greater problem.

The easiest thing to do is to post your material. You can build up a newspaper and broadcasting mailing list with the names and addresses of contacts. With a bit of anticipation many, if not most, stories can be prepared in advance and mailed to the national press and magazines. This is where an embargo may come in useful, so that you can allow two or three days for the post to reach London. You won't be too popular if the Widcastle papers receive their copy by hand on Wednesday when the story was in the *Daily Telegraph* on Tuesday.

The main disadvantages of the post are that you have to prepare the material and commit yourself well in advance (embarrassing if the WI speech is then cancelled through lack of interest!) and it means entrusting your precious material to the vagaries of the postal services.

The lazy but expensive way is to let a professional mailing house (directory again) do the whole job for you. They charge pretty painfully for each 'address', but are reliable and effective.

Some of the motorbike despatch firms now do 'runs' at so-much-per-address based on a mailing list supplied by you. They are usually quick and reasonably priced.

Depending on the number of staff you employ there is much to be said for sending a trusty employee down to London to grab a taxi and deliver the press kits or releases to each building. It may be expensive but it is the most reliable method and one of the quickest.

London is, of course, not the only place in the world, so if you live in the provinces remember other dailies like the *Scotsman*, with a head office in Edinburgh and an office in London. Also the big dailies have regional offices and can receive copy there. Still in London, there are some big newspaper groups who own and service large numbers of local papers from their central offices, such as Associated Newspapers, the Thomson Organisation and United Newspapers. These groups also provide syndicated news services to other newspaper groups.

Last, there are the news agencies who feed their own material to the national and other papers. If they like your story they will change it around slightly to justify their existence and then feed it out on a wire network to their many subscribers. The Press Association (PA) deals mostly with the UK press, while Reuters services financial customers in addition to distributing material worldwide. And there are others.

If you want to export there are scores of London offices of foreign newspapers which will certainly be interested in your material if it affects their particular countries.

To cover all the national and foreign newspapers, magazines and agencies is a massive task and one which is not to be recommended. It is best to start small, dealing only with the main nationals and, say, the Press Association and the regional group which is nearest to your own patch. Then look through a press directory sometime to see who else you should be talking to.

To sum up, then: newspapers — especially local ones — are the backbone of the media. Every time you do something in business try to get into the habit of asking yourself: Will this make a newspaper story? And if so, how?

Instead of just reading newspapers for information, look at them with a critical eye and ask yourself what makes them tick. What sort of material do they most use? What length and style are the news items? Then treat them as an opportunity to tell their readers about yourself and your company.

Don't be afraid of them. They need you as much as you need them.

Chapter 4
Television and Radio

Newspapers may be the 'bread and butter' methods of communicating, but they can't touch the broadcast media for impact. Television and radio have a glamour of their own. This is especially true of television, and as a nation we devote far more time to staring at the damned thing than we do to reading newspapers.

One good plug for your product can plant itself in the captive brains of millions. One snide remark on *That's Life* or *Checkpoint* and years of hard work can go down the drain.

Incredibly, most businessmen live in fear and ignorance of these two pieces of electronic hardware which are in every other way a part of our daily lives. Television sets proliferate in homes, offices, hotels, even cars and briefcases. Radios find their way into every walk of life from the bathroom to the remotest beach.

Both give you a heaven-sent opportunity for getting your message across. Imagine getting an item about the leftimug on to *Tomorrow's World* or John Dunn's radio programme. Just think of all those left-handed people drinking clumsily from right-handed mugs as they watch or listen . . .

See for yourself. In the course of a week's viewing and listening make a note of the number of times a product or an idea gets an airing before millions, often tens of millions, of potential customers.

To get an idea of how highly the big companies rate television, for example, look at the staggering amounts they will pay to advertise. Even on a local programme you are talking in thousands of pounds per 'slot', while a few words and a jingle which are 'networked' at peak viewing time can cost £100,000.

But why pay for it? The opportunities for free coverage

are there in plenty. First, though, there are some groundrules to learn.

Understanding TV and Radio

Just as the best way to get a feel for newspaper PR is to read through the newspapers with a more inquisitive eye, try to see behind the screen when watching 'serious' television. Try to understand how editors, researchers and interviewers operate. Then, when the time comes, you will be more familiar with the medium, less frightened of it and therefore more likely to succeed.

Look at programmes from the viewpoint of how they could help your own publicity. When you see a businessman appear on a programme ask yourself:

- ☐ How did that person get all that coverage? Did he go to them or did they come to him?
- ☐ Did he create a good/bad impression? Could he have done better? If so, how? Did the programme give his product/company/cause a fair deal? If not, was it their fault or his?
- ☐ Was he properly prepared and briefed, and how did he handle the interview? (We'll look at these techniques shortly.)
- ☐ Should I go on this programme, and how do I set about it?
- ☐ What sort of people make the programme? What makes them tick? What sort of material and people are they looking for?

The same questions apply to radio, of course.

The basic reasons for getting involved with TV and radio are the same as with other media. In fact, there are many similarities between a newspaper and its talking equivalent.

Read an issue of a newspaper and compare it to a day's TV and radio. All three give you the day's news, weather and sport. They all have their own light entertainment in the forms of cartoons, humorous articles and comedies. They have features and documentaries about everything from politics to the family life of the ring-tailed lemur. With the staunch exception of the BBC, all are largely financed by advertising (and even the mighty Beeb is finding it increasingly hard to do without).

Above all, newspapers, magazines, television and radio programmes are all run by journalists. They have their own editors, specialist editors, and general staff, almost all with the same original schooling in local newspapers.

In many ways, then, you are dealing with the same sort of beast. But, having got to grips with newspapers, there are some important differences:

- ☐ The deadlines are more immediate and frequent than those of a newspaper.
- ☐ The audience is much more demanding. We don't usually sit down with three newspapers on our laps, switching from one to the other if the bit that we're reading doesn't come up to scratch. Yet that is just what we do with television. If you fail to interest the viewer when describing your latest product he will simply dispose of you at the touch of a button.
- ☐ It's even worse with radio. With no picture to watch, the listener is usually doing something else — painting the house, planting the geraniums or driving along in the car. His mind will soon wander away if you don't make the leftimug sound like the most exciting thing since the internal combustion engine.
- ☐ Because the audience is different, the broadcasting journalists have to make the material more entertaining. When you are interviewed by a newspaper the questions, however tough, can be asked in a civilised fashion and you can ponder your answers. But on TV and radio there is much more cut-and-thrust and your answers have to be short, sharp and instant.
- ☐ Something happens to your personality when it's processed through all that machinery and transmitted through the air to someone's receiver. Without realising it, much of our communication is visual — with eyebrow raising, smiles, frowns, shifting of the eyes, gestures. On television these normal characteristics can give you a completely different look; on radio, of course, they don't appear at all.
- ☐ There is something terrifying about a studio. All those lights, microphones, cameras and gadgetry are enough to terrify the strongest person, not to mention the nerve racking knowledge that what you are about to say and do is going to be seen and heard by millions of other people.

Within the growth in radio and television broadcasting, probably the biggest development area is the coverage of business. For years business was the nonentity of broadcasting, the sort of thing for a handful of frosty old retired colonels to snooze over

'there is something terrifying about a studio'

in the television lounge of an Eastbourne hotel. Then the first few pathfinders like the *Money Programme* crept into the studios when no one was looking and transmitted after everyone had gone to bed. Now they are popping up like mushrooms. In addition to business and finance programmes, the usual current affairs and news programmes have discovered that industry and commerce can really be rather interesting.

It is an uphill struggle. Almost everything which makes for successful business — secrecy, caution, planning ahead, busy diaries — is inimical to what is needed for TV and radio programmes. Whatever criticisms we may have of the people who make the programmes it cannot be denied that they have to be lively and entertaining or people will simply switch off.

Businessmen and broadcasters mix about as well as tomcats round a dustbin. The former are traditionally reluctant to communicate while the latter almost never come from business backgrounds. Neither side wants to understand the other's problems. However, now that the broadcasters are doing so much more to give business a fair crack of the whip the onus is on the businessman to be more forthcoming.

This means treating radio and television as an opportunity for some positive publicity. Like their newspaper cousins, the journalists of the air are always on the look-out for new material, which could be your product, your business, your service. And just as there are ways of getting to know and understand how newspapers work, so it's worth spending some time learning about TV and radio.

Appearing on TV or Radio

First, it should be realised that there are quite a few differences between television and radio, apart from the obvious one that television shows a picture and radio doesn't. The broad principles are the same. As with newspapers, the broadcast media are there for you to communicate with your company's audiences. The principles of preparing a brief are the same, too, but after that you are dealing with two surprisingly different animals. Experience with television will help you to do better on radio and *vice versa*, but it's rather like being an experienced horseman and then getting on a camel for the first time.

We have already looked at how television does strange things to your personality. What appears on the screen can look very different from what you are really like in the flesh. Michael Parkinson told in the *Sunday Times* how he was surrounded at a book signing session by a group of middle-aged ladies who had simply come to stare at him. After a long while one turned to the other and said: 'Tell you what, Mabel, he doesn't suit daylight does he?'

But with radio there is only your voice to give any clue to your whole personality. Beauty, ugliness, physical composure and mannerisms count for nothing. This is a big advantage for radio. As another star said: 'The trouble with television is that the pictures get in the way.' If you think about it, that's very true. People actually *listen* to the radio. So long as it's only playing music the radio is fine for background only, but once the talking starts the listener tends either to switch off or to listen to the words. So you have a more attentive audience than you would have for many television programmes.

At the same time the absence of pictures means that you must be that much more lively. On television you can communicate some of your enthusiasm through your posture, gestures, eyes and expression, but on radio there is only your voice. So it's important to sound enthusiastic about your subject. Remember that the listener hasn't heard it before so throw some effort into it. Vary the pitch of your voice, too.

Listen to the people who succeed on radio: the interesting experts and entertaining presenters. What is it about them that makes them come over so well? Usually it is their sheer enthusiasm for the subject in addition, of course, to things like humour, knowledge and interesting facts. Notice, too, that if you have a regional accent it can be an advantage over a standard BBC-type voice.

For the most part, radio interviews are that much friendlier too. I am not saying that all TV interviews are punch-ups and all radio ones a friendly chat, but just observe for yourself. Maybe it is because there is so much blood and violence on TV, or maybe it's because each television channel is competing more for the viewer's attention, but, whatever the reason, radio interviews are less disposed to deliver below-the-belt punches than their television counterparts.

Radio and television studios are very different places. A radio studio is generally smaller and also more distracting. When you do a television interview the bright studio lights tend to isolate you and the interviewer from the rest of the world so that it is easier to concentrate on the message.

On television you are also less conscious of the small clip-on microphone, whereas in the radio studio you will usually sit at a desk with an enormous microphone stuck right in front of your nose. You can see the production team behind the glass panel, people are coming and going, and it is that much harder to remember what you were going to say.

If necessary you can spread any notes and reference papers out in a radio studio because the audience can't see them, but don't rustle them. Avoid other noises such as tapping the table with your finger or clicking a ballpoint pen.

The biggest difference between radio and television is that there are many more radio stations than television ones. There are more than 80 in Britain and the number is growing all the time. This means that they are hungry for news and always looking for items of local interest. Most local stations cover quite small areas, so you stand an excellent chance of getting some air time. Regional television stations cover bigger areas and there is thus more competition for coverage.

Contacts

Radio and TV are really only talking newspapers and, as with the press, personal contacts are important. It is not enough just to send a press release and hope they'll send a crew out or invite you in for an interview. The chances of success will be much higher if you ring somebody up and give them a good reason why they should be interested in your subject.

They are less likely than the local newspaper to want to meet you just to make the acquaintance, so wait till you have something to offer. There are four possible contacts:

☐ Programme editor
☐ Producer
☐ Reporters
☐ Researchers.

All have their advantages. The editor is the equivalent of a section editor in a newspaper. He or she may be a bit above taking a personal interest in the leftimug but is the person with the most influence. Much the same goes for the producer, who is responsible for putting the programme together, while the editor decides on policy and content.

Reporters are useful contacts, but can be hard to get as they spend a lot of time out of the studio. Probably the best contacts of all are the researchers. Often the programme really starts with them. Although they are near the bottom of the ladder when it comes to pay and decision-making, their job is to be the programme's antennae and to point the rest of the team in the direction of good stories.

They are usually more approachable and available than most other types of contact. However, the main thing is not so much *who* you contact as the fact that you contact *somebody*.

Like most journalists, the people who run radio and television are much more amenable than you might think. If you telephone the station and ask to speak to, say, the producer or editor of a particular programme you will almost always be put through to him or another member of the team who can advise you. Names can be obtained from programme details in *Radio Times* and *TV Times*, credits after the programme, or by ringing the station and asking who the relevant person is. A useful source of information is: *The Blue Book of British Broadcasting*, available from Tellex Monitors Ltd, London WC1X 8PR.

Don't be afraid of sending press material to national programmes, but for the most part it's the local ones who are likely to bite at stories about small businesses. All the stations, channels and leading contacts are listed in the main directories, so include the broadcast media in your deliveries and mailings of press releases. And don't forget IRN (Independent Radio News), which is based at LBC, London's independent station, and supplies the national news to all the local independent radio stations. They won't come to press conferences as often as the press but should always be invited just in case. Add a note explaining that separate facilities have been laid on for filming and recording.

Chapter 5
Preparation and Briefing

To Go or Not to Go

It's happened. You have just had lunch and are getting stuck into the afternoon's work. At first you think the voice on the phone is a friend pulling a practical joke: 'Hello, my name is Ruth Less. I'm a researcher for the *Look Round* programme. We've heard about the new factory you're building and I wonder if you could do an interview?'

Other than shouting 'Help!', what's the first thing to do? Well, for a start:

Ring back
This researcher is trying to push you into an instant decision. Would you say yes or no on the spot if it was a business transaction? It is best to get the basic details and have a quick think, so be businesslike — ask Ms Less some questions:

- ☐ Who will be doing the interview?
- ☐ How long will it take?
- ☐ What time do you want me for?
- ☐ Where?

Write down the answers. Now, unless you are absolutely certain, tell her: 'It looks possible, but I'll have to call you back. Give me just five minutes. Can I have your phone number?'

This has given you a few minutes of vital breathing space. Use it, but don't go mad . . . many a person has lost the big opportunity by saying yes too late. Devote those minutes of breathing space to making a quick decision on how you are going to respond.

Rationalise it

1. *Are you available or aren't you?* If not, could you *make* yourself available? If you can't do it tonight, is there another time that you could? Or could you go in and record the programme some other time today when you *are* available? If you really can't make it, is there someone else you could send?

If the answer in all cases is no, then you have no choice but to apologise — *and tell them honestly why you can't make it*. Be sure that they know you want to help and that they can try you again.

The trouble is, if you're successful enough at business to be wanted by the TV people then you're probably permanently busy, and it might mean cancelling an important engagement.

But if you are going to take this TV business seriously, then a lot of things which would normally be good reasons for not going are simply no excuse for turning down a chance to put your case over to a few million people.

It is more likely that, by fair means or foul, you can make it. If so, what next?

2. *Do you want to do it?* Put it on the scales:

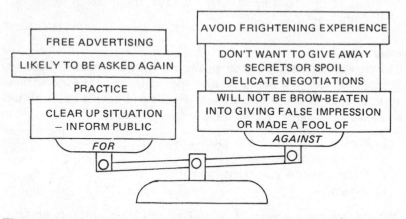

The scales *should* tip in favour. If they don't, *give them a bit of a nudge* — if only for one reason: the most chilling sound, one of the most damning things that can happen to you, the undoing of years of hard work, is the sentence: 'A spokesman for the company would not comment.' When you hear those fearful words after refusing to talk, you will wish that you had put your fingers on the scales when making that decision.

'So', you ask, 'if I've already decided to accept, what was the point of weighing the pros and cons in the first place?' There are two reasons:

(a) If you first convince yourself that it is right to accept, then everything that follows can be tackled with much more enthusiasm because you know *why* you are doing it.

(b) There just *might* be a genuine reason for saying no. It is unlikely, but it is better to have checked than to find out halfway through the interview.

Tell Them of Your Decision

While you have been weighing the pros and cons, Ruth Less has been thumbing through her contact cards for alternative interviewees, so get back to her right away. Tell her that you will do it — and now it is time to get something in return for the favour. It is essential to be firm with these people because they are in a business where liberties are bound to be taken. People who are approached by TV programmes tend to fall into two categories:

(a) those who are aloof and intransigent — so the TV people end up saying 'to hell with you, we'll get someone else', or

(b) those who let themselves be pushed around and would stand on their heads and bark so long as it pleased these gods of the silver screen.

The secret is to aim between the two extremes. Most TV types are reasonable, down-to-earth journalists. Only a very few are looking for trouble, but until you know the individuals better and can relax a bit (or get tougher), treat them all in the same way — like business acquaintances. It pays to be friendly but to guard your speech. It *never* pays to try to outsmart them.

Ask them
You have a right to be a little demanding — after all, you are effectively going into a business contract with them.

You already know where and for how long. Now ask:

☐ *Why* are they doing this programme?
☐ Why *me*?
☐ What is their source of information? If it's a press cutting, ask them to read it to you so that they don't confront you later with an unexpected piece of information.
☐ In what context will my contribution be used?

☐ Is it to be live or recorded? If recorded, how much of my interview will actually be used in the final programme?

☐ Will they be using any film or props that you should know about?

☐ *Who else* is going on the programme (such as a competitor or customer)?

☐ Can they give you an idea of the questions?

They won't give you a list of the questions word for word, of course. The exact form of the questions is usually only decided at the last minute, and if the interviewer finds an interesting line of discussion during the programme, it is his job to probe further and forget the original questions. Besides, if you know the exact questions in advance you're heading for one almighty boring interview.

There was an example on British television some years ago where the interviewer was facing a famous and ponderous architect. He wrote out his five questions on five cards and gave copies to his subject to prepare answers. At the last second the producer cut the interview from five minutes to three. It made sense to the interviewer to head straight into questions three, four and five. To his horror the architect mechanically intoned his prepared answers to questions one, two and three. If nothing else, the interview had a touch of originality to it!

However, they *should* have an idea of the *sort* of questions they want to ask. Television interviewers are professionals. So are their research teams, and they will be already thinking about their line of questioning. This at least will give you an idea. If they say (and they often will): 'Oh, we haven't really worked out our questions yet' (probably true at that moment), then say you'll ring back in half an hour to get an idea. There's no law to say they have to give you an idea of the questions, but there is some moral obligation to do so.

Once you have the line of questioning, don't treat it as gospel for they may well deviate, usually for genuine reasons. But at least you now have a guide.

Shock horror

'Thanks a lot', says Ms Less, 'we'll see you at six o'clock tonight. Goodbye.'

Click.

The feeling is not unlike watching the judge donning his black cap.

Consolation: it grabs everyone like that. If you *don't* feel nervous — or at least apprehensive — about doing the programme, then ask yourself very seriously if you're the right person to be doing it. The biggest clangers are dropped by the people who think they know it all. Even experienced campaigners should get that slightly sick feeling. It is best counteracted by filling in the time with thorough preparation. Now:

Prepare, Prepare, Prepare . . .

And again prepare. There is no such thing as over-preparation.

Never, but never, attempt to 'play it by ear'. You will be crucified if you do. In some ways it is disadvantageous to do a programme on your own specialist subject, because it is one thing to know an enormous amount about a subject and quite another to have your mind ordered and equipped to present that knowledge.

Try it and see. Take your favourite subject, buttonhole a friend and impart your knowledge of it, without preparation, in two minutes, in the most effective way you can. Now do it again with another friend, having first planned what you are going to say on the basis of this chapter. Then test your friends to see which one grasped the most!

Ideally you should allow at least an hour of preparation. Even if they want you at once, you *must* take a few minutes to get it all clear in your head. Get a taxi round the block, hide in the lavatory, anything, but never rush straight into the studio, like a sacrificial virgin, with a blank mind and a hitherto unblemished record.

As the seconds tick past it becomes increasingly difficult to put your thoughts in order. Dr Johnson said that a hanging concentrates the mind wonderfully. In many respects a television interview may *seem* like a public hanging, but it certainly doesn't concentrate the mind. The temptation is to do anything *but* concentrate on a thorough, well-rehearsed brief.

Think

Now, with time to get ready for this thing, sit down, shut the door, take the phone off the hook, and *think*. The first thing to get into your head is: *you are not going there to defend yourself*.

No matter how friendly the programme, be it face-to-face, phone-in, panel, down-the-line, film or whatever, at some stage you will find yourself feeling you have to justify your existence.

☐ 'Surely, Mrs Smith, this is all a bit unnecessary, isn't it? . . . '
☐ 'Mr Jones, it could be argued that . . .'
☐ 'We, the public, would like to know why you . . .'
☐ 'This is all very well, Mr Doe, but . . .'

and so on. The friendliest interviewer has at least one devil's advocate question on the notepad. But, as you will see later, this is not a court of law or a friendly pub you are going to. It is a communication medium with rules of its own. So start saying it now: *I am going there to say what I want to say, not what they want me to say.* And keep saying it.

Tell the good news

Let's look at a couple of practical examples:

A businessman building a factory causes all sorts of problems — pollution, unsightly buildings, noise and the like. A programme about that factory is bound to mention these problems, but the person being interviewed has a different story to tell. The factory is providing jobs, paying rates and taxes, making an exciting new product — all beneficial stuff.

Or take a pressure group — say the director of a feminist group. Is she going there to defend herself against accusations of being a bra-burning pain in the neck? Or is she going to use those three minutes to tell a couple of million other women that they are being treated unfairly and must make a stand against male piggery?

The most elementary grounding in public relations tells us how to concentrate on the good news and play down the bad. But the minute they feel the heat of the studio lights on their cheeks and hear the interviewer's distant voice, a lot of people forget this elementary principle and start to try to justify themselves.

It's so easy to forget, too, that although *you* know the good points of your company or organisation, the other 3,999,999,999 on this earth do not.

Plan the message

Having thought what it is you want to say, it's time to think about *how* to communicate it. Write down your basic argument.

Say, for example, you are a vegetarian. You now have this opportunity to encourage a few million others to become vegetarian too. Your knowledge of the subject is vast. There is a wealth of things that the simple carnivore should be taught —

economical vegetarian diets, suffering of animals, cholesterol damage, flavour and thousands of other things.

But now the requirement is to condense all this knowledge into a basic message. *At best you will get three points over.* These might be:

1. Vegetables are better and cheaper than meat.
2. Animal food is bad for you.
3. There are not enough animals to go round.

These points are now to be the basis of everything you say during that interview. Whatever the questions, whatever the angle, you want to get these points over to the viewer.

At this stage subsections can be added, for example:

1. Vegetables are better and cheaper.
    (a) Vegetables are half the cost of meat.
    (b) Vegetables contain all the protein and nutrients you need.
    (c) Vegetables are healthier because they contain roughage.
    (d) You can grow them in your own garden.

2. Animal foods are bad for you.
    (a) They contain large amounts of cholesterol.
    (b) etc.

By the time you have finished there should be three main points, each supported by three or four subpoints. If you know your subject you should be able to use that skeleton to get the main points of your message over in a couple of minutes — or to hold out for hours if you have to.

The important thing is: *each of those three main points must be able to stand up on its own*, because you might only have a few seconds in which to get it over.

Three is the optimum number. It can quite happily be only one or two, but go for the lower numbers rather than the higher ones. If you have four or five points to get over you will need (a) a lot of time, (b) a tolerant interviewer and (c) an abnormally receptive audience. By the time you start on point number four, most people will have forgotten what point number one (your most important point) was.

We shall look at *how* you get your points over in Chapter 7, 'Winning the Battle'.

Distil the message

In all that you work for and believe in there must be a basic message. You start with a whole philosophy and distil it. It can then be distilled again and again until there is just one drop of 200-proof liquor. Look at the years of thinking and millions of words and figures that have gone into brief phrases like: 'What's good for General Motors is good for America'; '$E=MC^2$'; 'There is no such thing as a free lunch'; 'From each according to his ability, to each according to his needs'.

In *Animal Farm*, the pigs cut their whole initial philosophy down to 'four legs good, two legs bad' and made the sheep repeat it until they got it right.

This is the principle to keep in mind when communicating something in a short space of time. And be sure to get this main message in *first*. Normally when we communicate, we start with the argument and end with the conclusion. But on television you have very little time, so you must get your (memorable) punch line in at the beginning . . . and then worry about the argument.

Limited time

It is human nature to try to communicate everything at once. Television, however, is like the stroboscopic lights on a rock group — a brief flash and you're gone. Next time you see an interview on television, watch for the amount of time the interviewee is given before the next question comes slamming in. What it boils down to is that you will have an average of about two minutes to say the *lot*.

Audience receptiveness

As well as having limited time at your disposal, you also have to contend with the state of mind of the people with whom you are trying to communicate. They are probably ironing, eating, reading, arguing, putting the kids to bed, thinking of changing channels. Even when the box has their undivided attention they are mentally relaxed and only concentrating at half power.

This means you have to keep it *very* simple. It is not that they are stupid — simply that they are switched off. Clearly, some people watch some programmes on a high mental plane, but as a general guide research shows that the awareness of the average adult viewer while watching television is that of an alert teenager.

So it is better to say the same thing several times than to say several things once.

Simple language

The only place you get prizes for long words is at university.

If you keep your words and sentences short everyone can understand what you're saying. This often requires more work than the long-winded stuff. Blaise Pascal once wrote at the end of a letter: 'I have made this letter longer than usual, only because I have not had the time to make it shorter.'

Too often we are guilty of being as out of touch as the judge in the famous Barnsley miner *v* Coal Board court case. Not convinced that the miner's injury was his employer's fault, the judge asked the plaintiff's counsel: 'Has your client not heard of *volenti non fit injuria*?'. He got the answer he deserved: 'M'Lord, in Barnsley they talk of little else!'

By contrast, the CBI succeeded with a campaign against the National Insurance surcharge — largely by changing the term to 'the jobs tax'.

We tend so often to use long words when shorter ones will do. As Robert Head, city editor of the *Daily Mirror* and *Sunday Mirror*, says: 'You don't shout "Copulate!" when you hit your thumb with a hammer!' Here he has compiled a list of the long words most commonly used by British management . . . with their much more effective, shorter equivalents:

A

accumulated	built up
acquired	bought (stole)
additions to	more
adequate	enough

B

Borrowings	debts

C

Category	class, type
commissioned	set up
confidence	faith, trust
connections	ties
considerable	big
constructed	built
contributing	chipping in
in cooperation with	working with
cost effectiveness	efficiency
currently	now
in the current year	this year

D

Demonstrate	show

89

discovered	found
disposed of	sold
division	part, side

E

expanded	built up, grew
expansion	growth
experienced	seen

F

facilities	works
main factor	reason
fifty per cent	half

I

increase	rise
individuals	people
institutions	banks, insurance companies, pension funds
interim	half yearly

L

liquid resources	cash

M

for the manufacture of	to make
marketing	selling
minority interests	partners

O

operations	business
operational	running
organisation	company, firm
overcapacity	glut

P

pharmaceuticals	medicines
pretax	before tax

R

reduction	cut, fall
representatives	salesmen
is responsible for	runs

S

satisfactory	good
surplus	profit

T

taxation	tax
turnover	sales

U

UK	Britain
United States	America

Anecdotes

Here come the real weapons in your armoury. Which of the following statements has more impact?

☐ Animal fats are bad for you and can be fatal.
☐ A friend of mine died from eating animal fats.

The latter actually gives you a picture of some poor devil dying horribly from indulging in non-vegetarian activities.

Or, to get back to our business context, which of these do you think the viewers will relate to more?

☐ The new factory will improve local employment.
☐ Albert Jones bought his friends a drink today for the first time in three years; that's how long he was out of work before our factory was built.

The first one may be shorter, yet it has less impact than the second, because the latter makes you stop and listen.

This is because *people love stories*. Possibly the greatest communicator of all time was Jesus Christ. His philosophy is still grasped by hundreds of millions of people in all languages, 2000 years after his death — because he said it all in stories. For example, if he had just told people to have a care for those they did not like, the homily would have been forgotten by morning. So he told them about a Samaritan — a baddie — who took pity on a mugging victim. And the message still gets through today.

The examples are many. Look at the complex analysis of human relationships and attitudes contained in the short and simple story of the prodigal son.

So back to the brief. Point 1 was: vegetables are better and cheaper, supported by: vegetables are half the cost of meat.

You could now make this read: vegetables are better and cheaper. Vegetables are half the cost of meat (wife . . . shopping). Because you are going to get that point over by saying: 'Do you know, last night I was on my own and felt like a treat, so I bought half a pound of steak, and it cost me a fortune. Now tonight my wife has got delicious baked potatoes topped with cheese and celery — for her *and* me *and* all four children, for *half* what that steak cost me.'

The point is that people *listen* to stories. They are also easy to *tell*. You know the story, so you don't need notes — and you put more life into telling a story than intoning a statement.

And a story is more difficult for the interviewer to interrupt.

Ideally it should be a true one, though it may be necessary to stretch things a bit to get the point over more forcibly. No one can challenge something like the wife and the vegetables, but beware of telling whoppers. If you're caught out once, you've lost your credibility for the whole interview.

Analogies

Another effective way of communicating is to ring a bell in the other person's mind with something with which he or she is already familiar. Again, Christ was the master at this. How hard is it for a sinner to get into heaven? — as hard as it is for a camel to go through the eye of a needle. Or what better description of a false prophet than a 'ravening wolf dressed as a sheep'?

The most complex things can be reduced to simple ideas, and good analogies are ideal when time is short. Let's look at a few examples:

The editor of *The Times* was explaining (in his newspaper, actually, not on television) the highly complex theory of the relationship of the money supply to inflation over a period of time. Not easy, but hands up those who can't understand the following 35 words: 'The money supply is like a tap attached to a hosepipe which is two years long. Once the tap has been turned on at one end nothing can stop it coming out at the other.'

Or take the case of a spokesman for a pressure group to improve rail travel. He was deploring the fact that British Rail had bought a load of new engines costing hundreds of thousands of pounds each and then had no use for them. Instead of groping with meaningless figures he simply said: 'Do you realise that every one of those engines is a new primary school rusting in the sidings?' Immediate impact. No one feels very angry about a redundant railway engine, but when it is put in terms of children deprived of their education everyone gets emotional about it.

And that new factory we were talking about: do you tell the viewers that it's 8000 square metres — or 'about the size of a football pitch'?

The rules are simple. Look at every item in your brief and ask if it can be grasped immediately by a newcomer. Can it be improved? Can it be put into everyday terms? Does a reservoir contain 123,455,200 gallons of water or does it hold three weeks' supply for your town? Does the factory have an unpleasant aroma of sulphur dioxide or does it smell like bad eggs?

The 'So what?' test

Finally, go back through everything you intend to say and subject it to the 'So what?' test. It may be terribly important to *you* . . . but what about Fred, sitting there in front of the box with a glass of beer in his hand, putting his feet up after a hard day?

Put yourself in his shoes — or pretend you're a sceptical interviewer — and ask yourself 'So what?' after each point you want to make.

Learn the brief

So far so good. The first part of the preparation time has been spent thinking out why you are going on the programme, what it is you want to say and how to say it. There is always a temptation at this stage to say, 'Right, I've got that taped, now I'll go and have a drink.'

Hold it. We're only halfway.

You know that terrible feeling when you have the answer to a question — it's on the tip of your tongue — but you cannot quite find the words or remember the details? Well, picture yourself in the same situation, sitting under the lights with the cameras relaying your embarrassment to the watching world.

This will not happen if you know your brief so well that a relevant passage springs to mind. We will soon be looking at how to get that particular message over regardless of the questions, but a fat lot of good it will do if you cannot remember what it was you wanted to say in the first place.

How long you spend boning up depends on how good your memory is, but you should not be satisfied until you know the brief by rote. You won't *deliver* it by rote, of course. But if you know exactly what to say and how to say it, you will be much more articulate . . . and it'll be a life-saver if you dry up in the studio.

Angle

News always seems to have an 'angle' — which is a position from which you only see part of the picture. Centuries of experience have taught journalists that people get bored with the whole picture, while a slant gives the story more interest. Many authorities are at work finding ways of presenting news and other programmes more fairly and in greater depth, but they have not found the answer yet. Hence this book.

The classic story about angle is the one about the Pope visiting London. As he arrives at his hotel the reporters flock round and flood him with questions. One hack asks 'Your Holiness, what do you think about the fact that there are rumoured to be call-girls in this hotel?' Horrified, the Pope asks '*Are* there any call-girls in my hotel?' Next day's headline: 'Pope's first question — "Are there any call-girls in my hotel?" '

It might seem a bit late at this stage to start worrying about their angle, but it has been left till now because *your* stuff is a whole lot more important than *theirs*, and also because you can never know for sure which way the interview will go. It's like an exam — if you try to prejudge the questions you might get it right and do well, but if you get them wrong you are in trouble.

So the best order of events is to be clear in your own mind about what you want to say, then mentally to prepare some responses to certain potential questions.

There are two ways of getting an idea of the questions.

1. WHAT THEY SAID THEY WOULD ASK
This is why you asked Ms Less why they are doing this pro-gramme and what they were going to ask. Her reply might have been: 'We think it's an interesting story and will be asking you how much it's costing, what the local reaction is, what good it's going to do, your firm's accident record — you know, that sort of thing.' Up goes the red emergency flare. The angle here is that your factory is about to come under fire.

How much different would your answers be if she said: 'Oh, we want our viewers to know more about your operation. We'd like to know more about the product, how many jobs you'll provide, what sort of profit you expect from it, and such-like'?

It's simple *your answers will be exactly the same*. That's what all the preparation was for, wasn't it?

But it helps to get an idea of the *trend* of their questions. Again, compare it with a business deal: when you go into a meeting to discuss a contract you like to know in advance what sort of reception you will get. The product you are selling is the same. The price you are asking is the same. But you will by instinct go out of your way to anticipate what the atmosphere at the meeting will be like and what sort of questions they are going to ask.

2. PUT YOURSELF IN THEIR SHOES
They have a job to do. Your job might be making money, promoting a cause, or running the country. Theirs is to entertain and inform a lot of people. Consistently. The interviewer and the interviewee will usually have different aims for the interview. Both are trying to use the same airtime for different purposes.

This thing you want to present on television — factory, theory, philosophy or whatever — pretend for a moment that you know nothing about it, yet you have the job of presenting it to the public by interviewing someone who does know something about it.

You will want to delve into what makes this person (ie you) tick. Is it a good thing? a bad thing? Will it affect the way we live? What are the viewers going to think about it? Will it affect our health? our pockets? our sex lives?

Looked at this way some questions are virtually dead certs. Say the target is our friend the female liberationist:

- ☐ What do you hope to achieve by this movement?
- ☐ Are women really downtrodden? Do they need help?
- ☐ How many members does your organisation have?
- ☐ What does your husband/lover think of this?
- ☐ What makes you think you are the right person for the job?
- ☐ What's your organisation going to do — in practical terms — to achieve these aims?

Or that factory:

- ☐ What will it manufacture?
- ☐ Why are you building it? Why now?
- ☐ How big is it? What will it cost?
- ☐ Is it necessary?
- ☐ How long will it take to build?
- ☐ Is it going to make a lot of noise? smoke? smell?
- ☐ Will it have sports/social facilities?

So, a list of potential questions is a valuable guide and an important part of the preparation. Having thought some questions out, you again have to remember to *keep off that defensive hook*. Just as an appetiser for the next chapter, where we are going to learn how to use those questions to our advantage, take that sneaky question to the women's libber: 'What makes you think you are the right person for the job?' The temptation is to give a straight answer about why you think you are the best person to do it, thus the *defensive* answer might be: 'Well, I've spent my life campaigning for women's lib. I graduated in sociology and have written two books on feminism . . .'

Now just where was all that nonsense in your prepared spiel? Nowhere, if you had any sense. The *positive* answer, in which you use the question to say what you already prepared, looks a little different: 'We downtrodden women *must* have a strong leader who will fight for our cause day and night. Men are dominant and arrogant — there was one in the paper yesterday, for example, who kept his wife in a dog kennel . . .'

Spot the difference?

Know Your Programmes

Some programmes bite more than others. Some are very fair and highly informative, while a browse through the annual findings of the Broadcasting Complaints Commission (HMSO) will show that one or two programmes do get rather carried away by their quest for 'truth and justice'.

Say you are approached by a heavyweight specialist programme that you know to be thorough and responsible. You must still prepare thoroughly and watch for pitfalls. They may, for example, say in all honesty that they are doing a programme on computers in factories and would like to feature your system . . . only to find in their investigations that some firms (guess who?) are buying the wrong equipment and not using it properly.

But by and large you will be happy to cooperate with them and participate in an in-depth interview.

On the other hand, you may be called by an 'investigative consumer' programme saying that they would just like to come along and have a chat about your employment policies, do some general filming, that sort of thing, nothing to worry about . . .

If you had seen the same programme a couple of weeks before lay into a hapless company like a pack of hyenas tearing up a half-dead wildebeest, then you will know to watch out!

This is why it is essential to know your programmes. Watch television carefully and critically. Become familiar with the different programmes and their different approaches. And familiarise yourself with the different interviewers. Then you will know what you are letting yourself in for.

By watching television in an analytical, questioning frame of mind you can also develop a feel for what makes a good or bad interview.

When you're watching a TV interview, ask yourself:

☐ How did he/she get on that programme?
☐ Is he/she doing a good job?
☐ What are the programme makers looking for?
☐ Could *I* get on that programme?
☐ How would I set about it?

Before Going On . . .

Dress and looks

This is less important than you think. Sure, people look at you on TV, but then people look at you in the street or on the bus. Most people dress the way they want others to see them. Do you look in the mirror in the morning when you dress? If so, you are already preparing yourself to go in front of the cameras.

So wear what you feel at your best in, what you want others to see you in. Preferably look smart. The main thing is to feel at home in your clothes. If you wear a suit to work, wear one to the studio.

There are, however, just a few tiny technicalities:

1. Don't wear stripes or checks — particularly narrow ones; they have a stroboscopic effect and appear to be moving.
2. Equally disconcerting is flashing jewellery, tie-pins etc.
3. Keep off clashing or really loud colours (especially red, which 'bleeds' at the edges).
4. Almost black and off-white are OK (a bit drab, perhaps) but *never* wear straight black and white. It sends colour cameras bananas — as anyone with a home video camera will know.
5. Take a quick check in the mirror before going on. If you want to appear a straightforward, decent sort of person — which 99 per cent of interviewees should — then it does not pay to display things like stray hair, slipped tie knots and smudged mascara. The make-up people in most studios take care this doesn't happen, but it is amazing how many times people manage to appear looking as though they have just been pulled through a hedge.

Transport to the studios

Sometimes the studio will send a car for you, in which case the onus is on them to get you there in time. If they can't manage a car, then get a taxi or go by chauffeured car. Only drive there yourself as a last resort; it will take up vital extra minutes finding the place and parking.

Be absolutely certain in advance where the studios are. Many TV companies have studios all over the place, and nothing is guaranteed to cause disaster more certainly than arriving late, or even at the wrong place. Plan to arrive at the studio in plenty of time — at least a quarter of an hour early.

Final touches to brief

Having prepared your brief, condensed it and memorised it, what you now do with it is up to you. It is probably best to avoid the two extremes of either (a) throwing it away or (b) going to the studios clutching a mountain of papers.

There are differing schools of thought on whether or not to use your notes in the studio, and if so, how to use them. This is discussed in more detail in 'Winning the Battle'.

Ideally, your basic points should be able to be contained on a postcard. Don't try to take loads of notes into a studio as directors don't like huge sheafs of paper messing up their carefully designed sets (contrary to belief, tabletops in studios are not designed to put things on and directors can be very fussy!). Also, it makes it look as though you don't know your own business.

My personal preference is for a small transparent folder containing a few relevant papers and the final version of the brief. Then on top of the pile goes a list of the points to be got over, with the really key points marked with a red dot from a felt-tip pen. There is no time at all actually to *read* your notes during an interview, so the dots (kept to a minimum) help the eye to zap in on a vital point at an awkward moment.

Example of a final brief

X TV *Look Round*
Vegetarian interview
Interviewer — Cliff Hanger

1. Vegetables better and cheaper
   — ½ price of meat (wife ... shopping)
   — all protein requirements
   — healthier — roughage
   (example of a fit vegetarian)
   — grow them in own garden (fun!)

2. Why animal foods bad
   — cholesterol (dead friend Joe)
   — impurities (fertiliser poisons)
   — bad for teeth

3. Ecological
   — increasing human population
   (500 new humans born during this interview)
   — decreasing animals
   — suffering
      — rearing conditions (describe calf in pen)
      — slaughtering conditions (describe slaughterhouse)

Checklist

PREPARATION

1. Decide whether to do it or not. Ask them:
   ☐ who is doing the interview?
   ☐ when?
   ☐ where?
   ☐ how long will it last?

2. Decide:
   ☐ are you available?
   ☐ do you want to do it?

   Weigh up the plus and minus points, but be inclined
   to answer 'yes'.

3. Ring them back. You'll want to know:

☐ why are they doing this programme?
☐ why me?
☐ what is the context?
☐ will it be live or recorded?
☐ any films or props?
☐ who else will be on the programme?
☐ what questions will they ask?

4. Prepare — at least an hour.

☐ Say what *you* want to say, not what *they* want
you to say;
☐ Plan the message:
   — 3 points (distil them, time is short) supported by
   — 3 or 4 subpoints each.
☐ Use:
   — anecdotes. Tell it in stories.
   — analogies. Ring a bell in the viewer's mind.
☐ Learn your brief — parrot fashion. Then you will
always have *something* to say.

5. Anticipate their angle. Likely questions can be
deduced from:

☐ what they said they would ask.
☐ putting yourself in their shoes.

6. Remember — keep off the defensive. You are going to
use *their* questions to get over *your* message.

DRESS AND APPEARANCE

☐ Be your presentable self.
☐ Avoid narrow stripes and checks.
☐ Avoid flashing jewellery etc.
☐ Never wear black and white.
☐ Check at last moment for stray hair etc.

Chapter 6
The Television Studio and What to Expect

Reception

Many egos are deflated when they arrive at a television studio. After the preparation and build-up, it is a degrading experience to arrive at the studios and find that the receptionist (a) is occupied with some other call or visitor when you arrive, (b) has never heard of you, (c) does not know that you are expected by a production team and are about to broadcast to millions, and (d) couldn't really care if you went up in flames. Soon, however, someone from the production team will come and collect you, and after a bewildering trip through corridors like the bowels of a ship, the next stop is usually the green room.

The Green Room

This term has come down from the theatre, where it refers to the bare, seedy, airless room which acts as a buffer zone for performers going and coming from their hour of strutting and fretting on the stage.

A television green room usually has comfortable chairs, a TV set for monitoring the programmes, and a well-stocked drinks cabinet — but it still performs its old theatrical role as a decompression chamber to adjust the body and mind for the next stage.

Your time in the green room will depend on how long there is to go before your interview. You might have to spend half an hour there or you might not see it at all. It's also quite common, depending on schedules, to go back afterwards, when a friendly outfit will often play back the interview on a monitor.

Meet the interviewer

This is a good time to ask to see your interviewer and producer if possible — to go over the ground. This is important. Interviewers are usually anxious to meet their subjects and talk about the interview in broad terms, but don't take 'no' for an answer the first time if at this stage they tell you that you can't see your interviewer until he or she is throwing the first question.

OK, sometimes the interviewer will be so busy he can't get away, but you owe it to yourself to insist on seeing him.

What do you talk about? Ask again about the *line* of questions. He will usually give you an idea, because by now he has an idea of what he's going to ask. Like you, he's not going into the studio intending to play it by ear. Most times he'll tell you and most times he'll try to stick to it, but there are two traps to watch for:

1. He has a perfect right during the interview to ask something completely different. It may be something you say, it may be sudden inspiration on his part, or maybe he is trying to catch you out, but it's all in the rules. Hence the stuff earlier about anticipating questions but not relying on them wholesale.

2. It's a good idea at this stage to 'educate' him in your subject — *but not too much*. The aim should be to ensure that the interviewer knows what you're about, so that crossed wires are avoided and the interview has more purpose. But most people have an overwhelming temptation to talk at length about the points they want to make, the questions they'd like to be asked and how they intend to answer them. This is two-edged. It can sometimes stimulate the interviewer into thinking 'Yes, that's interesting, I must ask that.' But more often it can smack of being a hobby-horse and cause him not to ask you that question at any cost. So the best advice is not to reveal your hand — especially before a contentious interview.

Unguarded talk

This desire to tell all to the interviewer in advance stems from a deadly tendency to want to off-load on someone when under stress. You know those Gestapo films: first the beatings and torture, then the relaxed chat with a friendly 'doctor' who offers you a cigarette and gets you to confide in him. He's the 'soft' interrogator, and that's what television people become in the green room or studio before a broadcast.

Watch for the warning signs. Listen for yourself saying:

☐ 'Actually, this isn't in my notes but ...'
☐ 'I'm not going to say this in the studio, but ...'
☐ 'I shouldn't really tell you this, but ...'
☐ 'This is off the record, but ...'

Nothing is off the record. There is no law, written or unwritten, whereby even the kindest interviewer can't drag up some whispered confidence and throw it straight back at you, live, in front of the cameras.

So the simple rule is to be friendly, talk about your subject by all means, joke, chat, but *never*, at *any* time, before, during or after the show, in the green room, white room, black room or bathroom, say *anything* to *anybody* that you might afterwards regret.

Drinking

The trouble with alcohol is that it's pleasant stuff and relaxes the nervous system. It can't be denied that a couple of drinks before a programme can unwind you, but who said anything about being unwound? That's just what you *don't* want to be. *They* would love to have you sitting back in your chair, relaxed, smiling amiably, coming out with a few witticisms and occasionally opening the cupboard door ever such a tiny bit for a quick peek at the skeleton.

To hell with what *they* want. *You* want to be alert, articulate, on the ball. People think it's impossible, but you can film the most seasoned drinker before and after a small drink and there can be a marked deterioration in clarity and concentration in the second film. Drinks are best left till after the interview when you can drink the cabinet dry if they'll let you, so long as you still keep the lid on those secrets (and there's no danger of them wanting to do a retake just as you're cracking your third bottle!).

Nerves

The craving for a stiff drink at this stage is enhanced by the fact that you're shaking like a leaf. At least, you should be. If you don't experience that slight breathlessness and inverted stomach then it is time to start worrying, because over-confidence can be lethal.

Almost everybody, including seasoned interviewers, feels some tension before going on, and for a first-timer it is usually petrifying.

Good. Don't fight it. *Use* it.

Many experts recommend things like yoga, deep breathing, transcendental meditation and other tricks. But all that adrenalin is useful stuff. It makes you alert, lively, punchy, and it's a shame to lose it.

In the minutes before a boxer goes into a fight he's a bundle of nerves, but the moment the bell goes the nerves vanish. A television interview is just like that. Be a little masochistic for once and learn to enjoy the tension and use it to your advantage. In short doses it's good for you and makes a change from the humdrum of business, housework, the daily routine.

Make-up

Shortly before the programme you will be made up to prevent the cameras doing horrible things to you. Make-up experts are well used to nervous customers and are good value for a friendly chat. They know what they're doing and are best left to pat powder on your cheeks and put hair in place. Of course, if it looks like you are being transformed into Count Dracula then say so, but you should find make-up a nice little interlude.

You're on Next!

From make-up they will either lead you straight into the studio or back to the green room for a few minutes. Either way . . . *you're on next!*

Checklist

- ☐ Ask to meet the interviewer — and producer if possible — to discuss the *line* of questions.
- ☐ Let him know what you're about, but don't give too much away.
- ☐ No confidences; *never* anything 'off the record'.
- ☐ Stay off the booze.
- ☐ Enjoy that nervous feeling. Use it to your advantage.

Chapter 7
Winning the Battle

Sorry about the military terms. But in a way it *is* a battle —
with yourself, with them, with anyone who disagrees with your
cause or your business.

The Terrain

The battleground is the studio.

It looks more like a nuclear war has occurred — chaos reigns.
Technicians beaver away with cables, plugs, filters and things.
People rush around with clipboards and shout instructions at
each other. There are bright lights, cameras, microphones. And
in the middle of it all is a small oasis of calm — the seats where
you and your interviewer are to slug it out.

Who Does What

Editors, producers, directors, floor managers, researchers,
cameramen, secretaries, not to mention deputies and assistants
to them all — it's not worth worrying at this stage about
who's in charge. It varies from country to country and from
programme to programme.

It is fairly safe to assume that the person making the most
noise *between* takes is the producer, while the one making all
the noise *during* takes is the director. It's best to intercede
through the interviewer if you need anything.

This applies to all the distractions like clapper boards and
people making masonic-looking signs at the interviewer to tell
him that he's got 10 seconds before take-off or that the programme ended five minutes ago.

Let *them* do the worrying. If they want you to do anything

they'll soon ask you. If you want anything just ask the interviewer.

Take Your Seats

Again, let *them* show you to your seat and do all the fussing. For the technician who slings the microphone round your neck, or clips it to your lapel, nothing is more infuriating than a fumbling interviewee trying to assist.

The only thing you need to fuss with once you've sat down (and I promise this will be the last military analogy) is a final check of your 'uniform'; a quick touch over the head and across the forehead for stray hair, straighten up clothes. Pull the back of your jacket down to stop it riding up behind the collar.

Now, *sit forward*. Perch on the edge of the chair if possible. The difference is remarkable. If you sit in this slightly tense position you *feel* alert and, more important, you *look* alert throughout the interview.

Voice test

You know how maddening it is when you have to keep changing the volume control on your set? Some nights you wouldn't believe it, but in fact the studio has someone doing the 'sound mixing', in other words, trying to make everything leave the studio within a certain volume range.

They ask you to do a 'voice test' by saying a few words to see what your voice does to the needles on the sound mixer's console. Their favourite is to ask what you had for breakfast or lunch.

Here's a chance to make them happy right from the start. Virtually everybody either booms out their voice test and then starts the interview *sotto voce*, or they whisper the voice test and then launch into the first question like Billy Graham at a revivalist meeting. The former loses you the first few words while the mixer turns the volume up, and the latter makes millions of TV sets shudder while he frantically turns it down.

So give the voice test the same impact as you intend to use during the interview. The director and sound mixer will be delighted.

Good side/bad side

We're almost ready to start. First, though, it's important to think about how the viewer sees you. The horrible truth is that if he or she doesn't like your manner anything you say will be lost. All of us tend to be put off by someone who looks slick, shifty, scruffy or stupid on the screen.

It has nothing to do with being handsome or ugly. In fact the smooth looker often starts at a disadvantage.

It's all to do with the subtle difference between looking alert and looking nervous, between endearing mannerisms and infuriating tics, pausing for emphasis and gaping open-mouthed, appearing a 'character' and looking crazy.

For one thing, almost everyone has one profile that is more pleasing to the eye than the other. Look at photos of youself, look in the mirror (preferably between two mirrors placed so as to give an accurate image), ask your relatives and close friends. It's not vanity to try to show the 'good' side to the cameras — it's an intelligent way of giving the best impression you can.

Of course, don't spoil the interview by thinking of nothing other than which side of your face the cameras are pointing at, but if you can develop a feel for your best image it will go some way towards winning over the viewer.

Where to look

Forget the cameras and look at the *interviewer*. If you try to look into the camera during an interview it appears contrived, and besides, you stand an even chance of looking into the wrong camera. A red light on top of the camera lights up when it is on, but even experienced newscasters often play Russian roulette between the red lights. There is no way of knowing when the director will order a different camera to cut in.

So *look at the interviewer*. Talk to the *interviewer* and you're talking to the *viewer*.

Speech

Forget the old 'rain in Spain' stuff. The only thing to remember is that your voice is going through all sorts of electronic gadgetry before hitting the ears of someone not accustomed to the way you speak. So speak *clearly* and distinctly — a little slowly if you're a fast talker — but otherwise in your normal voice.

If you have a strong regional accent it's a *plus point*. Don't hide it.

Gestures

The days of sitting on your hands went out decades ago. If you want to wag an accusing finger at the interviewer, do so. If you feel like turning your palms up and saying 'My life, what a question!', go ahead. The only things to avoid are fussy or nervous movements. This goes for:

Mannerisms

A quick scratch on top of the head, rubbing an eye, cleaning a pair of spectacles are really quite human. They can even be used to good effect. For instance, a genteel blowing of the nose can give you five seconds of vital thinking time in a tight spot (ten, if you carefully fold the handkerchief and put it away).

Again, though, beware of nervy and irritating habits. Don't drum the table, fiddle with paper-clips or bite your nails.

Anxiety and nervousness often show themselves in twisting hands. If you are nervous, and most people are, then most of the time you can either keep your hands clasped together or rest them quietly in one place; but don't be afraid of natural gestures. Do not cross your arms as this is very off-putting. Also, be aware of where your microphone is placed; if it's attached to your blouse or shirt, don't brush it or bang against it as it will make very embarrassing noises. If it's a floor-standing mike, don't keep crossing or uncrossing your legs as you will bang it.

Smoking

No. Definitely no. Some people do smoke in the studio, but it is distracting, slovenly and messy. Those wisps of smoke floating across the screen can be infuriating. And strange things can happen. In one interview (fortunately it was in a training session), the subject lit a cigarette half-way through. He did so while the camera was on the interviewer, so the viewer had no indication that a cigarette had suddenly appeared on the scene. The subject took an enormous drag on his cigarette, and at that moment the camera cut back to him, in close-up, for an answer to the interviewer's question.

The effect was extraordinary. This apparently normal man, half-way through a successful interview, opened his mouth to speak and belched out smoke like Puff the Magic Dragon. The smoke poured out. It came out of his mouth and nostrils. It even seemed to come out of his ears. His otherwise excellent answer — and the rest of the interview, for that matter — was lost for ever on a hysterical audience.

Smiling

Some say do, some say don't. On balance, smiles should be

treated with caution. For one thing, they can make you seem a big smug, and there is always the danger, in a recorded interview, of the edited tape or film showing your cheerful, smiling face just after an edited-in serious question or accusation. Appearing to beam from ear to ear when asked your opinion of an earthquake in Peru is not guaranteed to enamour you to the viewer.

However, it's not worth worrying about too much. A naturally cheerful person should not be prevented from smiling, and a naturally sour type certainly shouldn't use his first TV interview to learn to grin.

Notes

Lastly, there's the question of what to do with your notes. People have more hang-ups about it than most other aspects of interviewing or public speaking.

Many people use notes or reports as security blankets, arriving at the studio with a great pile of them only to be reduced to a nervous wreck when they are asked not to take them into the studio. But there is no reason on earth why you shouldn't have a notepad on your knee or in front of you on the table. It can actually give you quite a professional look, especially if it conveys the impression of your being armed with plenty of facts and figures.

The great big golden rule is *not to read from them*. If the camera catches you peering at your notes in a frantic search for the answer to the last question, then you have blown the interview. You just won't seem credible to the viewer any more.

Hence those headings and red dots in the brief. With any luck, if you prepared properly, you can look the interviewer in the eye throughout because it's all in your head. But if you get stuck, then you can give yourself a prompt with no more than a quick glance.

Sincerity

The last, and most important, thing is to be sincere and *enthusiastic* throughout. Television can be a deadening medium, so an interviewee needs to 'hype up' to come across 'normally'.

Horror Story

So much for the preliminaries. Let's get started on the interview.

Suddenly, it's all about to happen for real. A voice calls out '30 seconds' — and you and the interviewer stop talking and look at each other like two waxwork dummies for what seems an eternity.

Then he speaks, and the cameras are recording.

Your head is now on the block. In the next few minutes it is in your power to promote yourself, your company or your cause to immense advantage. Or you can make an utter fool of yourself. It's up to you.

Let's now create a victim and look at a duff interview. The characters and every aspect of the script are borrowed from what happens in real life — from different interviews at different times, in different words. Though fictional, our interview is certainly not impossible.

We have a typical interviewee — a businessman — and a typical interviewer. They are male only for convenience, and a businessman has been selected as one of the vast group of people who are likely to be asked to do an interview, yet who have the least experience in television techniques. But the things we are about to see — the questions, the tricks, the pitfalls, the missed opportunities — apply to us all, male, female, of all ages and walks of life.

The story so far

Oscar Winner is chief executive of Basket Eggs, a big poultry and egg producer. The company has announced plans to build a plant at Foxtooth, a town of 100,000 inhabitants. It will be one of the biggest companies in the region, and the local TV station has brought Winner in to be interviewed on the evening current affairs programme.

The interviewer, Cliff Hanger, is a seasoned pro. In real life he's a nice guy, with a wife and four children. He holds doors open for old ladies in supermarkets and feeds the ducks on a Sunday afternoon. But he's a bit cynical about businessmen and has one fault; if he thinks someone is a baddie, or is trying to pull a fast one on him, he goes in for the kill.

He's told Winner about his line of questioning, but has been pretty vague — 'What will the factory do?', 'How much will it cost?', 'Any particular problems?' etc.

Winner, for his part, is completely confident about the interview. There's nothing he doesn't know about chickens, he's a good after-dinner speaker and his wife thinks he's handsome. He's so calm about it, in fact, that he got in a quick nine holes at the local golf-course before going to the studios.

It's 6.30 pm, and the interview is going out live. Hanger launches into his introduction.

Here's the script. Most of the studio directions are omitted for simplicity, and the numbers are inserted for reference when we analyse the interview afterwards. Read it through in one go before going back through the numbers.

Hanger: Our next guest on the programme is someone who has a lot to answer for. He's Mr Oscar Winner *(cut to Winner sitting back (1), smiling, arms folded)* who's to build a poultry plant on the outskirts of Foxtooth. The type of plant planned is to be like the one in this film. *(Film: 45 seconds, showing rearing of chicks and battery conditions, some birds dying, most losing feathers etc) (2).* Mr Winner, why are you bringing this kind of thing to Foxtooth?

Winner: *(3)* Well, it's a logical decision. The company is expanding and Foxtooth is an ideal location for a new poultry plant. In fact ...

Hanger: *(4)* But we've just seen how senseless suffering is caused to countless thousands of chickens. Why not buy a field here and let them fly around a bit?

Winner: *(5)* Ah, that simply wouldn't be economical, Cliff *(6)*. On a free-range basis you need a square-footage-to-bird ratio of 14.7:1 on grade A feed, and more on lower quality grain *(7)*.

Hanger: Are you saying that you practically torture helpless birds, simply because it's more profitable that way?

Winner: Well, it's hardly torture *(8)*. I'm just saying that all the people watching this programme ... *(9)*.

Hanger: We all know, though, that your method produces lower quality eggs *(4)*. In the film they showed a waste-burning unit; are you going to bring one of those here?

Winner: *(5)* Oh yes. That's standard equipment in this sort of plant.

Hanger: But that chimney in the film was belching filthy black smoke over the neighbourhood. Now you're telling us that we're to have a factory chimney polluting the atmosphere *(10)*.

Winner: Well *(11)* I should like to reassure the viewers that the

111

chimney will only produce about 120,000 cubic feet of waste smoke per hour *(pause) (12).* And it won't be burning all the time, of course *(pause).* I mean, you can't run a plant of this sort without some waste smoke *(pause).* Besides, er . . . *(13) (pause)* this sort of production requires a certain amount of recycling and waste-burning and so on *(14).*

Hanger: All the same, 120,000 cubic feet sounds like an awful lot of black smoke for a small town like Foxtooth. Tell me, Mr Winner, how long is the plant going to take to build?

Winner: Just under a year, we hope, though the first eggs should be in production on a limited scale within nine months. We've got a really good firm on the job, and once it's finished it'll be the most modern plant of its kind.

Hanger: Who's building the plant for you then?

Winner: I . . . *(15)* Why do you want to know? *(16)*

Hanger: It would be interesting to know if it's a local firm. The construction industry round here has been going through a rough patch lately, hasn't it?

Winner: Has it? *(17)* I must admit I'm not using a local firm . . .

Hanger: Why not?

Winner: Well, quite simply because we've chosen Stackbricks to do the job.

Hanger: Why Stackbricks, though?

Winner: Well . . . I mean . . . *(angrily) (18)* look, why are you asking me all this stuff about the builders? You're making me sound as though I've been bribed or something! *(19)*

Hanger: *(coolly)* OK, so it's a year from now and you've built the factory. What benefit are we going to get out of it?

Winner: Well, I think *(20)* the great advantage of the Winner system is that you get more eggs for less money. Everything is automatic so we can cut costs and provide a cheaper egg by the thousand.

Hanger: I see. Do you have enough eggs for export, then?

Winner: Oh yes! We even sell frozen eggs to the People's Republic of China!

Hanger: I'm glad to hear it. That's Mr Oscar Winner, who's going to build a plant here to send eggs to China. What the people of Foxtooth will do for eggs is anybody's guess *(21) (cut).*

The lessons to be learnt

That interview took just over two minutes. In that time our friend Mr Winner put his foot in it at least 21 times.

OK, so the interview is a fictional one. Interviewers are not always as tough as Hanger, and interviewees not always as dumb as Winner. But many of those 21 points will crop up even in the kindest interview and, when you get the occasional tough one, all 21 will be dotted over the interview like land-mines.

Let's go back over the interview, point by point, and see why Mr Winner *didn't* make it. All the points are important, but five are golden rules (numbers *4, 5, 8, 16* and *20*).

(1) LOOK ALERT

It's terribly tempting to try to relax in a studio chair. This can make you look too contented — if not a complete slob. It's especially true if the opening gambit is an attack on you; the camera catches you sitting back, smiling smugly, and the viewer already wants to see the interviewer wipe that silly smile right off your face.

(2) ANY SURPRISES?

Remember back in the preparation you asked if they were showing any film? If they *are* using film you should insist on seeing it first. The same applies to surprise studio guests and any other gimmicks.

(3) SHOUT 'UNFAIR'

If they say it's impossible, or say there's no film and then spring it on you anyway, you must let the viewer know right away that *you* haven't seen the bit of film which *he's* just seen.

If your interview was recorded, and they then use film to your disadvantage, it's time to complain. (More on that later.)

(4) DON'T LET THE INTERVIEWER BUTT IN

In normal conversation we tend to stop when someone butts in. On television the reverse applies. *You* hold the whip hand, because there's nothing they hate more in the studio than two people talking at once.

If the interviewer cuts in before you've finished, *raise your voice — slightly but firmly and finish what you were saying.* He'll have to shut up or ruin the interview.

However, don't confuse making your point with waffle. *Always* finish the point you were making and then shut up.

Never go rabbiting on for more than about 15 seconds at a time.

(5) REFUTE INCORRECT STATEMENTS
What kind of a question was that? Here Hanger is using the oldest trick in the book — a derogatory statement followed by a different question. It's a favourite trick, so be on your guard for it. If the interviewer makes any statement that you don't like, jump in and put the record straight *immediately*. Then answer the question.

(6) NO NAMES
It's a small point, but don't forget that ultimately you're not talking to the *interviewer* — you're talking to the *viewer*. If you address him by name it removes you one stage from the person with whom you want to communicate.

Be especially careful of first names. They can make the interview sound a bit contrived or 'pally'.

(7) NO JARGON
That spiel about the 14.7:1 ratio may look ludicrous, but it happens all the time. People are so used to the gobbledegook of their everyday jobs that they forget the viewer can't understand a word of it.

Remember instead the advice in the briefing chapter about using simple analogies. (Example: a space expert in a recent interview explaining the nature and dimensions of the Soviet Soyuz space station: 'It fits together like a child's construction set. With the latest addition it's now about the size of a domestic garage.')

(8) DON'T DEFEND
Somehow on television it's as bad as an admission of guilt. *He* used the word 'torture': now *you've* used the same word again, which is just what he wanted.

Either go straight into your (already prepared) point about the benefits of battery breeding or, if you have to reiterate his loaded question, use it as a launching pad for a counter-attack. Indeed, far from being on the *defensive* in a television interview, you should go on the *offensive* — in the nicest possible way!

(9) THERE IS ONLY ONE VIEWER
He or she is an individual. He is not 'one' or the 'audience' or

the 'viewer'. You are speaking to him through the interviewer and it shouldn't be necessary to refer to him as anyone in particular.

Picture yourself in an *average* television-viewing mood. Even intelligent people tend to switch off mentally when they watch, and then you must allow for the fact that a typical audience covers the whole spectrum of education and taste, with the weighting towards the lower end of the scale.

A good tip is to think of someone you know in real life who to you is an average person in the street. It might be your mother, husband, wife, cleaning lady, postman or teenage offspring. Throughout the interview picture that person standing there in place of the nearest camera. You continue talking to Cliff Hanger, but really the person you want to get through to is that individual where the camera is.

(10) DON'T LET THEM MISINTERPRET

An interviewer will often paraphrase your message for you. It's usually done with good intentions to achieve simplicity, and if young Hanger has just put it better than you can put it yourself, then so much the better.

But if it's done to your detriment, put it straight at once.

(By now we can see that some numbers have repeated themselves. Alas, there's no law to stop you making the same mistake over and over.)

(11) WELL...

It's human nature to start with a 'Well . . .' It doesn't do any harm in small doses, but that's the third time Winner's started with 'Well' in five questions. He's losing impact.

(12) THE CALCULATED PAUSE

It's like when you put your foot in it at a party and want the floor to open up. You ask some lady how her husband is these days, and remember as you speak that he died last month. So you quickly burble some other nonsense to cover up and realise you're saying something worse.

The interviewer loves it. He loves it so much, in fact, that he won't always wait for you to say something stupid in the first place. He'll create a pregnant silence for you to fill — like your own grave. Watch for yourself how often a subject on television goes on talking because he feels he has to.

Yet here's a situation where you really hold the whip hand.

Say what you want to say . . . then shut up. The interviewer is only too conscious that if the interview is filled with long pauses he'll be chewed out by the producer for a boring piece. The onus is on *him* to keep things flowing. If he clams up suddenly and deliberately, be sure you've got one of your key points over, then sit there in silence and wait for him to crack. He will.

(13) ER, UM
It's worth some practice in everyday speech. The more you 'um' and 'er' and 'ah', the less certain you sound of your facts.

(14) AND SO ON AND SO FORTH AND THE LIKE
Meaningless. List your items and quit while you're ahead.

(15) HE WHO HESITATES IS SERVED UP ON TOAST
This may sound contradictory having just encouraged you to shut up in certain circumstances, and having talked earlier of ploys like cleaning your spectacles and blowing your nose in order to gain thinking time. But the crucial thing is not to let the *viewer* know that you're frantically thinking up the right answer! Stall intelligently if you have to, or launch straight into your response.

Incidentally, quite a good breathing-space technique is to ask the interviewer to repeat the question (though obviously it would look ridiculous after a simple question like the one about the builders).

In fact in this particular case Hanger's question is a sidetrack, and right now Winner shouldn't be answering the question at all, as we shall see.

(16) DON'T BE SIDETRACKED
Interviewers are always looking for a dark alleyway with a corpse at the end of it. (This is one reason for not relying too much on prepared questions and answers.)

A good interviewer can sniff trouble a mile away at the end of a sidetrack. If you give him half a chance he'll be off down it like a frustrated ferret — so it's your job to keep him on the main street.

The question of who's building the plant is of immense local interest, though you can see that Hanger hadn't thought of it — he got the lead accidentally from Winner ('We've got a really good firm on the job...').

From Winner's point of view it's a dangerous sidetrack and he compounds the danger for the next three questions before he spots what's happening.

It's a tricky one, this. Some successful interviewees, particularly politicians and trade union leaders, escape by simply not answering the question, but in this case the local viewer will soon realise that Winner's hiding something if he evades the question altogether.

He'll have to give a quick answer and belt back into the main street again. Let's see if we can get him out of it when we redo the interview in a few moments.

(17) KNOW YOUR GROUND
It should go without saying. Interviewers are usually backed up by research teams who ply them with facts and figures. If you *are* caught out, don't make it worse with a dumb retort like 'Has it?'

(18) STAY COOL
Never lose your temper. If you ever became really adept at being interviewed you might *pretend* to show great anger and indignation at the right moment, but that's outside the range of this simple book.

Stay as cool and professional as you can. Once you become ruffled the interviewer is half-way to the kill.

(19) DON'T VOLUNTEER THINGS
Winner has just done exactly what Hanger wanted him to do. Hanger knew he would be in hot water if he himself made any allegations of corruption, so he's let Winner imply the allegations himself.

We do it all the time in conversation — it's another of those crazy defence mechanisms. On the air it's as good as a confession of guilt. Don't make a rod for your own back by raising any subject which is irrelevant to your objective.

(20) BE POSITIVE
Terms like 'I think', 'It seems that', 'I believe' reduce a firm statement of fact to a personal view. Be assertive. Present your material as fact, not opinion.

(21) THE LAST WORD
Another favourite. See for yourself how often it happens.

Under the guise of 'winding up', the interviewer delivers the *coup-de-grâce* while you sit there open-mouthed and the clock ticks to zero.

In recorded interviews the detrimental, snide final comment is sometimes edited into the end, in which case it's an occasion for a complaint.

In a live interview, however, you again hold the whip hand if he slips in a derogatory remark, because you can utterly ruin his summary by shouting out and getting your case in last.

But you have to be damned quick. Come out with something like: 'That isn't true. I've already told you that xyz ...', so that they finally cut the interview with you reiterating one of your key points.

The key points

Winner's first and biggest mistake has been saved till now. *He went in cold, without a brief.* He failed to hammer any key points home — because he didn't have any key points to hammer home in the first place.

He made the cardinal error of playing the interview by ear because he thought he had all the answers in his head.

Now, for a spot of practice, why not go over Winner's interview and look for the main points he *should* have got over?

He wants to make it clear that Basket Eggs is good news. What are the positive points?

1. For a start, it must be demonstrable that eggs are beneficial or presumably one wouldn't eat so many of the things. This is a great time for Winner to be selling his product — to make the viewer want to go out and buy a dozen.
2. Second, a major investment in a plant can be shown to be a benefit to the community. Basket Eggs is sure to provide jobs, to add to the income from rates and to boost local trade.
3. And then there's the fact that mass production should make for *cheaper* eggs — that's good news for the housewife.

Of course, there are other points — those valuable exports to China, for example. But Winner should major on no more than two or three main points. The viewer simply can't absorb any more. Other points can be slipped in if there's time.

It's worth noting, from these three points alone, how quickly you can start to spot some of Hanger's irresistible nasties in advance. For example: there are plenty of experts who say eggs are bad for you; there's the fact that a new plant will destroy some piece of greenery; and what about those poor old hens?

In any case Winner should have come to terms long ago with the negative aspects of his business. It would be wrong to pretend that everything's perfect in business, and Winner's line of work is full of warts which it would be both immoral and impractical to try to hide. His job here is to highlight the good bits and play down the negative ones.

Getting the message over
Shortly we shall rerun the interview and see if winner could have got those key points over despite Hanger's loaded questions.

And here we come to the most important point of all: *you can make your points regardless of the questions*.

It's incredibly simple. There isn't a question in the world that you can't turn to your advantage.

Every question is nothing more than a peg for you to hang your case on. There are varying degrees. Some questions are 'gifts' and enable you to say what you wanted to say simply by answering the question. Most questions, however, require some kind of answer before getting on to your own material. Only as a very last resort should a question be ignored completely.

The principle of what it's all about is summed up by a real-life statement in a television interview by a trade union leader: 'Let me answer *my* questions first and then I'll answer *yours!*'

It may be taking things a bit far to put it in those words on the air, but that's the thought which should always be at the back of your mind.

The best way is to answer the question *briefly* and then move on to your own material.

Let's say, for example, that Hanger throws in a question about production: 'Just how many eggs a day will your plant produce?' A fair enough question. But Winner's first key point had nothing to do with the number of eggs; it was to tell the viewer that eggs are good for you and you should eat more. He knows his plant will produce 50,000 eggs a day — now all he has to do is to add a bit: 'Fifty thousand. That's 50,000 meals. One egg alone has enough protein and vitamins to keep you going for half a day.'

Well, Cliff Hanger is a seasoned pro and knows propaganda

when he sees it, so he quickly changes tack: 'According to some experts, eggs can cause heart failure — is this what you're advocating?'

But Winner hasn't finished selling his eggs. It would be a mistake to skip the heart failure problem altogether so he *uses* the question: 'Taken to excess, *anything* causes heart failure. But a couple of eggs a day are really good for you — and they're so versatile. They're delicious boiled, fried, scrambled and in omelettes.'

We caught a glimpse of this simple technique in the last chapter with our female liberationist friend who was asked about her qualifications for the job and *appeared* to answer the question with an attack on men.

It's something you can practise in your head, in three simple stages:

1. Think of something you'd like to say if you were given 15 seconds of free television time.
2. Think up the nastiest, most loaded, antipathetic question about the subject.
3. Put the two together!

Watch the pros doing it. Next time you see a politician getting away with murder, look for the techniques:

- ☐ 'Racial discrimination *is* a problem, I agree, and it has a bearing on what I was about to say ...'
- ☐ 'I can't really answer that question without explaining some of the background ...'
- ☐ 'Sure, some people say we made a mistake, but we mustn't let it cloud the real issue, which is ...'
- ☐ 'That's a good question and I'd like to return to it later. But just to dwell for a moment on your earlier question about ...'

There is no limit to the number of ways you can use a question for your own purposes. It's not like a court of law. There's no judge to rap his gavel and say 'Will you kindly answer the question!'

At the same time, though, many interviewers are getting wise to these evasion techniques — like the interviewer on *A Week in Politics* who responded to a load of old flannel from an MP with: 'You've answered my question obliquely. Now perhaps you can answer it directly ...'

Good interviewers are like terriers. They'll keep on biting at the same heel. So, once you've got out of a tight corner, don't breathe a sigh of relief and mop your brow. Save that for after the programme.

Eventually, Hanger will have to give up because he knows it's dull television to keep on asking one question.

Remember, though, that *evading questions is just a technique for tight spots* and getting your message over.

Too often, experienced perfomers find they enjoy evading questions so much that they do it all the time, just for the hell of it. Our friend the viewer may not realise what your game is the first few times, but you are eroding your credibility every time you refuse to strike a ball.

Let's say Hanger asks Winner how much profit he made last year. Winner knows he made a packet. And he knows Hanger knows it. This is a case for a 'perspective' answer, rather than evasion:

— 'Last year was an exceptionally good one, but let's get it in perspective. We made 30 million, but eggs are a highly risky business and with all the money we're putting into the Foxtooth plant we'll need all the cash we can get', or:

— 'It works out at a tenth of a penny per egg', or:

— At first sight it *looks* a lot — 50 million pre-tax in fact — but don't forget 20 million of that goes straight to the Government to provide schools, defence and welfare . . .'

(Incidentally, as sure as eggs is eggs, Hanger is only waiting for the *figure*. The moment Winner says 30 or 50 million, Hanger will leap in with: '*30 million!* Here you are making a killing while . . .' Don't let him get away with it. Keep talking and insist on making your point.)

Don't be afraid, either, of saying you can't answer a question if it's genuinely impossible. This is often the case during delicate strike negotiations, or where lives or official secrets are at stake. Say that you can't answer and briefly explain why. Then quickly return to one of your key points before the interviewer can open his mouth for the next question.

Success

Now it's time to apply the lessons to Winner's first interview. The story's the same. The people are the same, and to demonstrate how Winner should have dealt with each question we'll keep the questions the same:

Hanger: Our next guest on the programme is someone who has a lot to answer for. He's Mr Oscar Winner *(cut to Winner, sitting forward, intent and alert)* who's to build a poultry plant on the outskirts of Foxtooth. The type of plant planned is to be like the one in this film. *(Film: 45 seconds, showing rearing of chicks and battery conditions, some birds dying, most losing feathers etc).*

Hanger: Mr Winner, why are you bringing this kind of thing to Foxtooth?

Winner: *(1)* If you'd shown me the film before the programme I could have told you how out of date it was. It completely failed to show the immense improvement in the standards of egg production in the last few years *(2)*. The Foxtooth plant . . .

Hanger: But we've just seen . . .

Winner: *(3) (more firmly)* The Foxtooth plant will give a vital boost to what is probably the most important area of food production today *(4)*.

Hanger: But we've just seen how senseless suffering is caused to countless thousands of chickens. Why not buy a field here and let them fly around a bit?

Winner: If you'd shown film of a field of chickens you'd see why *(5)*. Next time you see a flock of free-range chickens, just watch them for a while. Their life is hell. You'll see that a few strong birds peck the others into a state where they're so miserable that they lay far less eggs than their protected sisters in a battery plant *(6)*.

Hanger: Are you saying that you practically torture helpless birds, simply because it's more profitable that way?

Winner: *(7)* All the evidence points to the fact that our hens have a safer and longer life and lay more eggs *(8)*. We can check them the whole time so we know that every egg which leaves our plant is good and wholesome.

Hanger: We all know, though, that your method produces lower quality eggs. In the film they showed a waste-burning unit; are you going to bring one of those here?

Winner: *(9)* Listen, our eggs have been tested side-by-side with free-range eggs and they are every bit as good. Do you realise that there are more protein and nutrients in one single egg than in any other foodstuff at the price? *(10)*

Hanger: What about this waste-burning unit?

Winner: Either you have a pile of chicken feathers a mile high or you process them *(11)*. As a matter of fact our process has a number of useful side products — manure, chicken paste, offal *(12)*.

Hanger: But that chimney in the film was belching filthy black smoke over the neighbourhood. Now you're telling us that we're to have a factory chimney polluting the atmosphere.

Winner: I'm telling you the exact opposite. It will produce no more smoke than half a dozen domestic chimneys *(13)* — and only occasionally at that.

Hanger: Tell me, Mr Winner, how long is the plant going to take to build?

Winner: The sooner the better as far as everyone's concerned! When this plant is in production it'll mean 200 new jobs for Foxtooth *(14)*. It's the biggest industrial investment in this region for years.

Hanger: Who's building the plant for you then?

Winner: *(15)* It's important first to look at the scope of the project. These new buildings will be the most up to date, safe and efficient in the world. We're investing a fortune to produce the best eggs at the lowest price.

Hanger: But it would be interesting to know if it's a local firm. The construction industry round here has been going through a rough patch lately, hasn't it?

Winner: *(16)* It has everywhere, I'm afraid, and of course we looked at the local building firms when we tendered. In this case we chose Stackbricks because of their experience of building this sort of plant. Next time you're in the Ducktown region take a look at the big, modern egg farm they built there ... *(17)*

Hanger: OK, so it's a year from now and you've built the factory. What benefit are we going to get out of it? *(18)*

Winner: *(19)* The biggest single benefit is that you'll get more eggs for less money. Everything is automatic so *we* can cut costs and give *you* a cheaper egg.

Hanger: I see. Do you have enough eggs for export, then?

Winner: Oh yes! We even sell frozen eggs to the People's Republic of China.

Hanger: I'm glad to hear it. That's Mr Oscar Winner, who says he's going to build a plant here to send eggs to China. Meanwhile, I wonder what the people of Foxtooth will do for eggs.

Winner: *(20)* They come first, of course ... *(cut)*

That's more like it

There's no such thing as a perfect interview, and that one won't go down in television history. But this time Winner made a good showing by applying some elementary techniques. With the same story and basically the same questions he got his key points over and dealt firmly with the nasty questions.

What's more, Hanger and his masters will be pleased with this more lively and informative interview, so the odds have improved on Winner being invited back for another go — when the factory opens, for example.

It's worth a look back over the interview to examine the ways Winner improved. This time he *scored* 20 times. We'll just run over the inserted numbers and see what lessons he learnt:

(1) He's making it clear to the viewer, right from the start, that he hasn't been given a chance to see the film. Not only does this stop him making a fool of himself but it also encourages the viewer to side with Winner over this unfair treatment.

(2) Then he immediately uses the unseen film as a bridge to stress the improvements in egg production.

(3) No nonsense. He hadn't finished speaking so he beat Hanger at his own game and cut in. Note that he does so firmly rather than loudly. You shouldn't have to shout.

(4) We're still at the start of the interview, but Winner's now got two points in already. He's used the 'improvements' bit as a peg for reminding the viewer that eggs are an important food product.

(5) In the first interview he was on the defensive over this 'suffering' accusation. This time he attacks by comparing it with the apparently greater suffering of free-range chickens.

(6) And by now he's telling a *story* — painting a picture for the viewer of a lot of chickens giving each other a rough time.

(7) Hanger won't give in on his 'suffering' angle. So Winner uses it to reiterate his view that his chickens are happier.

(8) He also realises, though, that Hanger is starting to sidetrack him with this 'suffering' angle. So, before Hanger can get started again, Winner bangs in another key point on the back of his 'happy hens' argument. He's starting to make the viewer feel like eating an egg.

(9) This is the nearest he gets to showing anger. Underneath

he's furious at Hanger's sniping, but that 'listen . . .' is firm, not angry, and he's really telling the *viewer* 'listen to *me*, not *him*.'

(10) And again he uses the moment to sell a few more eggs.

(11) It doesn't take much imagination to convert a simple reassurance about a waste-burning unit into an image in the viewer's mind of a pile of chicken feathers a mile high. Yet it doubles the impact.

(12) 'And while we're on the subject of waste-burners', Winner says in effect, 'look at all the other goodies you're going to get out of my factory.' His plug for chicken paste doesn't really have much to do with the waste-burner, but it only takes a few words to link the two.

(13) Here's a good example of an analogy. Gone are the 120,000 cubic feet and in their place are half a dozen domestic chimneys — which the viewer can picture at once.

(14) It's taken a couple of minutes for Winner to have a chance to get this key point in, but he's not going to let it go. Again, he uses the question as a bridge. If he merely answers the question 'How long is it going to take to build?', he'll never demonstrate the boost he's giving to employment in the region. The technique is *essential* and *simple*, but it requires constant practice.

(15) Winner smells obvious trouble in the question about the builders. It can only be trouble as there's no other reason for asking a dumb question like that. So he sidesteps the question, if a little crudely, and gets on with another plug. But this time it doesn't work. It's a reasonable attempt to evade the question, and he's gained some thinking time, but he realises that Hanger isn't going to let this one go in a hurry.

(16) So this time he says who the builders are, but quickly explains, honestly and rationally, the reason for the choice. Note his first response, by the way. In fact he doesn't know any more about the local construction scene than he did in the first interview, but 'it has everywhere, I'm afraid' shows much more apparent understanding and sympathy than 'has it?'

(17) Now he's painting a picture for the viewer again and starting, in effect, to describe what his new plant will look like.

(18) There are times to forget the rules, and this is one of them. OK, Hanger has interrupted again, but he also happens to

be changing the subject, which is just what Winner wants. So this time he lets Hanger carry on.

(19) Don't look a gift horse in the mouth! It's quite easy to be so much on the ball with interview techniques that you overlook a chance to give a straight answer to a straight question.

(20) It's not much of a rejoinder but he's got to be quick. At least he points out that Foxtooth will get its eggs, and he spoils Hanger's snide little wind-up.

Just a few rules. A few techniques. All of them very simple. Yet with a bit of preparation and practice the same person achieves a 100 per cent improvement.

One thing which doesn't show in a script is *sincerity*. This time round Winner has scored several points, but it's important to avoid being smug or snide when winning. It can be tempting to sit back with a satisfied smile, but this must be avoided at all costs.

The important thing is to show the viewer that you're winning, not to show him that you *know* you're winning.

Sit Still at the End

One last small point: many's the person who's finished an interview with an immense feeling of relief and blurted out something like, 'Phew, I thought you had me there, Cliff', only to find that the cameras are still live. Once the interview has been wound up, remain sitting, looking at the interviewer, until someone tells you it's over. Avoid the temptation to say anything or to jump up and walk out.

Self-assessment

Whether you watch on your set at home or on a studio monitor, try at all costs to see the interview at least once. Be really critical. Watch the replay of your interview in as detached a mood as possible and pretend you are a typical viewer seeing yourself for the first time.

Did you come over as a sincere, honest person? Did you as the viewer relate to the figure on the screen? Were you in charge? Did you sell yourself? Did you sell your cause or product?

Watch the interview with your brief on your lap and tick off the key points as they come over. At least half the page should be ticked and any point scoring two ticks is good news.

There is no better critic than yourself. If you can ever sit back with a contented smile on your face, then something is seriously wrong.

Checklist

Preparation

Let *them* do all the fussing:
□ show you to your seat
□ fix microphone etc

Last check on clothing:
□ stray hair
□ straighten tie, shirt etc
□ pull down coat at back.

Voice test — same value as you'll use in the interview.

Appearance and manner

□ Sit forward in seat, leaning slightly forward.
□ Use your good side, if possible.
□ Look at interviewer throughout.
□ Speak clearly and distinctly.
□ Use your hands as much as you want, and don't
  be afraid of mannerisms, *but avoid:*
  — fussy or nervous movements
  — smoking.
□ Have your notes with you if you want. Glance at
  them for reference, but don't read from them.
□ Be *sincere* and *enthusiastic* throughout.

Handling the interview

GOLDEN RULES

1. Don't let the interviewer butt in without a fight.
2. Refute any incorrect statements.
3. Stay off the defensive.
4. Don't get sidetracked.
5. Be positive. (*continued*)

Silver rules

1. Look alert.
2. Try to anticipate surprises.
3. Know when they spring something (eg a surprise film or studio guest) on you; let the viewer know.
4. Don't address the interviewer by name — remember it's the *viewer* you're talking to.
5. If the interviewer rephrases your statements, make sure he's got them right. If not, put them right at once.
6. Don't use jargon.
7. Remember there is only *one* viewer.
8. Avoid too many 'wells' at the beginning of your answers.
9. Don't feel you have to fill embarrassing silences. That's the interviewers job.
10. Stay off the 'ums' and 'ers'.
11. Don't tail off with 'and so on', 'and so forth'.
12. Only hesitate if it's deliberate.
13. Know your facts.
14. Don't lose your temper.
15. Don't volunteer irrelevant information.
16. Watch for the interviewer getting in a harmful last word.

Key points

The *platinum* rule is to think all the time in terms of telling your own key points to the viewer, *regardless of the questions and other distractions.*

Practise ways of getting points over:
☐ think of something you want to say
☐ think up a nasty question
☐ put the two together!

Self-assessment

☐ Watch the result as objectively as you can and see how you've measured up against this chapter.
☐ Check off the points on your brief to see how many you got over.

Checks and Balances

Broadcasters work within a system of checks and balances. The most obvious is that they work within a team of people: a researcher or reporter will report back to a producer, the producer to an editor and so on upwards. The composition and titles will vary from company to company, but in practical terms it means that everything that is broadcast will have been checked and rechecked.

And both the BBC and the Independent Broadcasting Authority (IBA) have guidelines for their programme makers which help to shape their editorial decisions.

Some important features of the IBA's guidelines (the BBC's are similar) are that:

☐ Whether an interview is recorded or live, interviewees should be made aware of the format, subject matter and purpose of the programme as well as the way in which their contribution will be used. Interviewees should also be told the identity and intended role of any other proposed participants in the programme.

☐ Interviewees should also be told that an edited version of their interview will be shorter and programme makers should take care that the shortened version does not misrepresent the interviewee's contribution.

☐ The context in which extracts from a recorded interview is used is also covered. An interview should not be edited so as to appear by juxtaposition to associate a contributor with a line of argument he would probably not accept and have no opportunity to comment on. Neither should separately recorded interviews be edited together so as to give the impression that the contributors are in actual conversation with each other.

But despite the guidelines, programmes will sometimes go astray and misrepresent you — intentionally or otherwise.

What then?

Complaints Department

As a general rule it's best to ride with the punches.

The more you appear in the media, the more they will get it wrong — but remember that almost all publicity is good publicity because over a period of time people have only a hazy impression of what they've seen and heard. What matters is that they remember your name, for studies by the MORI research organisation show that, contrary to the old adage, *familiarity* breeds *favourability*.

So try to look at the general shape of the wood and not worry too much about the individual trees.

However, there are times when enough is enough and a programme oversteps even the most generous bounds of journalistic licence. Then it is time to hit back, hard.

It should virtually never have to apply to *live* interviews. If they wipe the floor with you 'live' then you have only your self to blame.

Even so, there are occasional exceptions, the most likely one being the interviewer's wind-up. No matter how quick you are, there are times when an interviewer will slip in a final cutting and incorrect remark before you can open your mouth. The sound cuts out and you're made to look a fool.

If you are involved in a programme which messes you about — and you are actually in studio — take the first opportunity you can to point out the error, making sure that your correction is relayed to the producer as soon as possible, not just written down in a researcher's notebook. The IBA (and the BBC) instruct that misstatements of fact should be corrected as soon as possible — in the programme itself if live, or in the next edition of the bulletin.

If you are watching the programme at home or elsewhere, ring the television company directly. You will in the first instance probably be put through to the duty officer. Some are more helpful than others. If they do not say that they will contact the production team responsible immediately, insist firmly that they do and leave your name and a telephone number where you can be contacted.

If, however, you are in a studio taking part in a live interview in which the line of questioning is not what you had agreed, you can make that perfectly clear in your replies, even if you are interrupted.

Similarly, it is unlikely that they will spring a surprise guest on you, because they cannot afford a débâcle in studio on a live programme as this is as equally embarrassing for them as for you.

The best way to avoid unpleasant surprises is to ask beforehand who will be in the studio. Will it just be a straight interview or will there be an opposing opinion? If there is, think what you would be attacking yourself for if you were in their position — and make sure you have prepared some answers.

The most common complaint against television programmes, however, is against pre-recorded, non-studio programmes.

Documentaries and current affairs programmes of the *World in Action* and *Panorama* style are not normally instant reactions to news stories. They are researched and filmed over weeks or sometimes months.

It is usually against this type of programme, with which the participants can have a long association, from first being approached by a researcher or reporter to the point when the programme actually appears on the screen, that accusations of bias, unfairness and misleading reporting are levelled.

If you are unhappy about what has been filmed, get in touch with the producer. You cannot demand editorial control as you have, by your agreement to be filmed, entered into a form of contract. But, if you feel you have reasonable grounds to suspect that you were misled or that the material filmed was potentially damaging if not handled properly, speak to the producer in the first instance, and if still not satisfied find out if there is an editor of the programme who has overall editorial control.

If you are still not happy, contact the controller or director of programmes at the television station — without delay. At each stage be firm and ask for an immediate response, because once the programme has gone out the damage will have been done, whatever future action you take. In the case of the BBC, you can also appeal to the director-general.

If you are dealing with an ITV company which does not respond satisfactorily to your questions your last resort is the Independent Broadcasting Authority (IBA).

The IBA is the statutory body set up to regulate the ITV companies and Channel 4 and it has a duty to make sure that broadcast programmes maintain: 'a high general standard', 'a proper balance' and 'due impartiality' in matters of political or industrial controversy or relating to current public policy. It can, if necessary, order the re-editing of a programme before transmission.

However, if you have no inkling that something has gone wrong until the programme has been transmitted and you feel that the programme was inaccurate, misleading or potentially damaging, act immediately it has gone out.

Write in full with your complaint to the editor of the programme (if any), and the director or controller of programmes, and send a copy of your letter to the IBA in the case of an ITV company or Channel 4 and to the director-general in the case of the BBC.

Getting a response, let alone a correction, can take some time. If you want an immediate response to an ITV or Channel 4 programme, Channel 4's *Right to Reply* programme can give you an instant way of putting your case forward and challenging the producer responsible.

Right to Reply is a weekly programme which gives viewers a chance to air their views about what they see on the small screen. One of its main functions is to give individuals or organisations who have been involved in a programme and feel they have been misled or unfairly edited a chance to put their case in the studio.

The BBC is also planning to broadcast a programme along the same lines, recognising that it should have some measure of accountability to the public.

What if all else fails? Aside from legal action, the last resort is the Broadcasting Complaints Commission, Grosvenor Gardens House, 35 & 37 Grosvenor Gardens, London SW1W 0BS (01-630 1966).

The BBC was set up by the 1981 Broadcasting Act to consider and adjudicate upon complaints of unjust or unfair treatment by radio or television programmes. Complaints about programme balance, content, taste, standards and scheduling are outside the Commission's jurisdiction.

The workings of the Commission are slow as it takes time to gather all the evidence from both sides. In the first instance written evidence is submitted, with each side being requested to reply in full to the other's points. If it is then decided to proceed, the Commission has the power to consider complaints at a formal or informal session when each party separately gives oral submissions.

The only sanction available to the Commission once it has adjudicated on a complaint is for it to direct the broadcasting body concerned to publish an approved summary of the complaint and the Commission's findings. It cannot require a broadcasting body or programme contractor to apologise to the complainant or to broadcast a correction or provide a remedy.

However, it is the Commission's practice to direct the publication of each adjudication in the *Radio Times* or *TV Times* as appropriate. Copies of all the adjudications and summaries of what has been approved for publication in the *Radio Times* or

TV Times are also sent to the national and provincial press.

Radio interviews and programmes are covered by the same guidelines as television and the same complaints procedure applies. For complaints against independent local radio stations (ILRs) the final authority is the IBA, and for serious complaints against ILRs as well as BBC local and national radio, you can go to the Broadcasting Complaints Commission.

If you think things are so bad that you must take legal action, take it quickly, and use a lawyer with experience in this area or you can end up with a hefty bill for nothing. If possible, try to get an injunction to stop the programme going out. It's much better to prevent the damage being done than to try to clear up afterwards.

And *always* use a pocket tape recorder (with plenty of tape!) to record any filming and interviewing at the time it happens. It will show the programme makers that you are on your mettle and help you assess how fairly or otherwise you have been represented.

Checklist

Get it right in the first place! Brief yourself thoroughly to avoid pitfalls.

Establish *before* the programme:

- ☐ What type of programme it is.
- ☐ As many details as possible.
- ☐ Know your rights — BBC/IBA guidelines.

If filmed:

- ☐ Make sure the film crew is accompanied.
- ☐ Don't ramble. Be conscious of how your answers can be edited.

If unhappy with the way you are treated by a programme, be sure that you really do have a grievance, then complain to:

- ☐ Producer/editor. If still not satisfied:
- ☐ Controller/director of programmes. If still not satisfied:
- ☐ IBA or BBC director-general. If still not satisfied:
- ☐ Broadcasting Complaints Commission.

If it's *really* serious, take legal action — quickly — and use a lawyer with experience in this field.

Training Courses

If you have any intention of taking TV and radio seriously, a training course is a must. Several experts now run courses at which you can spend a day or two being put through mock interviews in their own 'studios'.

The greatest advantage is that you can see for yourself how you come over on television. It's one thing being told that you are too aggressive or that you have an infuriating habit of scratching your right ear, but the message never really sinks in until you've seen it for yourself.

Another advantage is that you can be put through some tough interviews in private. You can learn by your mistakes without those mistakes going out to a few million people. Costs and quality of training vary considerably. If you don't know of a good TV trainer in your area try your trade association or a representative body such as the CBI or Institute of Directors for advice.

If possible, go more than once. Being interviewed successfully is like flying an aeroplane. Having learnt the difficult business of flying you need regular practice to keep your hand in.

Ideas for Programmes

The rewards of using TV and radio as public relations tools outweigh the risks a hundred times. As part of taking a positive approach, ask yourself constantly if there is the germ of a programme in what you are doing.

Programme editors are always on the look-out for new material. Many items, and even whole programmes, start life as a small press cutting which an eagle-eyed researcher has spotted. If you invent something, manufacture or sell a new product, land a big export order or are being evicted for not paying your rates, remember the broadcasters in addition to your normal press dealings.

All they are looking for is something original, informative and entertaining. And make sure they know you are there if their programme involves your industry and they need someone to comment on a particular aspect.

Chapter 8
Surveys

'Surveys' is a dull-sounding word for a great PR device. The idea of conducting a survey into something might sound eccentric and remote, but in fact it provides two of the essential criteria for favourable coverage — credibility and a 'peg'.

Here's an eye-catching piece from a corner of a national newspaper:

> More than 80 per cent of families using private education are making sacrifices to cope with school fees. This was one of the main conclusions reached in a survey undertaken by X, a specialist in school fee planning.
>
> A random selection of 300 clients of X was designed to show the extent to which private education is imposing a financial burden, but also to provide the first-ever profile of the modern fee-paying parents, and to find out why they used private education.

And so it goes on for another six paragraphs. Notice that in the first two paragraphs the name of the firm is mentioned twice and the material will have caught the attention of anxious parents seeking advice on how to finance the cramming of some education into young Egbert's thick skull.

In other words, X came over as an authority in the business of advising on school fees, and gave the newspaper a reason for publishing the story. It was news. We tend to think of people who can afford private education as the idle rich. Yet here was proof that most of them were making sacrifices.

Or take this one:

> Nearly three-quarters of Britain's junior doctors — hospital doctors below the rank of consultant but including senior registrars — work more than the official maximum of 80 hours a week, says the British Medical Association.

Again there is that eyebrow-raising statistic and the stamp of authority. If either the BMA or the school fees company had simply issued press releases stating that doctors were over-worked or that parents needed expert help, they would probably have never got past the news desk. The fact that somebody has conducted a survey makes all the difference.

Sometimes a regular survey can help turn the sponsors into a national institution. Business people and bureaucrats up and down the country splutter their toast and marmalade over the CBI survey of business opinions each month, while the record-buying youth of Britain cause hiccups in the gross national product each time the 'top 20' is announced.

Advertisers often cash in on 'survey' material, such as 'Nine out of ten housewives can't tell toothpaste from soap powder', or whatever. And the principle is the same for forecasts and indices. Several times a day, for example, the *Financial Times* gets a free plug when its stock market index is announced on the radio news.

Surveys have many uses. They can steer a company in a particular direction after it has conducted a market research survey, or they can have a bearing on government policy. For PR purposes you might decide to 'create' a survey to prove your point or promote your product, or you might make some capital out of a survey which you have already conducted for some other purpose.

If you use a survey as a means to obtaining coverage it has several advantages:

1. It provides a natural 'peg' for the story. It turns a run-of-the-mill press release into real news. Remember that your press release will be vying with dozens of others for the sub-editor's attention, especially if you want national coverage. Other things being equal, the survey will always go to the top of the pile.
2. Once the reader has seen the first paragraph, he or she is more likely to keep on reading. It's the next best thing to spying on the neighbours over the garden fence. We have an insatiable appetite for news on what other people are doing. Survey information tells us about other people's tastes and activities, and where we fit into the picture.
3. There is nothing like a whiff of statistics to give your organisation an air of authority. A few boffins may get emotional about your 'survey base' and methods, but the vast majority of people will take it at face value. I am not

suggesting that you stop two passers-by who have heard of your product and call it '100 per cent awareness', but you can often get away with asking one or two simple questions of a few people and immediately assuming the credibility of scientific research.

'the next best thing to spying on the neighbours over the garden fence'

For example, the school fees people only sent, presumably, a simple questionnaire to 300 clients (and there is no mention of how many actually replied). Whether it was an inexpensive piece of 'grandmother research' or a costly professional exercise was immaterial to the reader. What mattered was the figures, which transformed a piece of special pleading into an authentic statement of fact. The concept is simple enough, but if you decide to conduct a survey there are some important points to consider.

First, while it is easy to get some sort of figures from the most elementary 'survey' (if one of your two kids likes chocolate and the other doesn't you could claim that 50 per cent of children like chocolate), if you want to get a truly representative reading it must be done by experts.

It takes years to learn the many techniques for getting an accurate reading. For all sorts of reasons, people simply don't give straight answers to straight questions, even when they think they are doing so. It takes experts to formulate the questions and solicit and interpret the answers. And to get a representative reading you need a wide 'survey base', ie you have to ask a lot of people.

This leads to the main disadvantage of a full-scale survey: money. Although the resulting publicity is free, the survey itself can be very expensive. Even fairly simple surveys, if conducted by experts, can run into thousands of pounds.

You must decide between a 'proper' survey or a home-made one. If you do it yourself it can still be used for publicity purposes, and for your own gut feelings about your customers or whoever it is that you are surveying. If you have the job done by professionals it might set you back a bit but at the end of the day you will have a valuable piece of market research in addition to the publicity.

Conducting a Survey

First you must decide just what you want to survey and why. There are endless possibilities. Try cutting some examples out of the papers and studying them to see what it is about them that makes 'news'. They can range from how many housewives prefer sliced bread to what percentage of people are going to vote for which party.

Here is an example from a magazine:

> Kiss me tender, kiss me sweet. If you kiss at all, you are probably between 16 and 44 years old, are a relative or child and live in the south west. In the west 78 per cent had kissed somebody on the mouth in a week. The other extreme was Scotland. Only 54 per cent had kissed anybody (on the mouth) in the same period. If you are the friend of a woman you will be more readily kissed on the cheek by 61 per cent of women, compared with 37 per cent of men.
>
> If you like kissing marriage isn't necessarily the key. In a week only three out of four married people had kissed. Only half the people Gallup interviewed in a survey for X mouthwash had bothered to do anything about their breath before kissing. Most people (65 per cent) rely on toothpaste, one in five uses mouthwash and 18 per cent use mints, these last being particularly favoured by people aged 65 and over.

Note how the product again gets a big plug from the survey.

The next stage is to think how a survey of some sort could help you and your business. Say you own a record shop. There are three other record shops in Widcastle and competition is needle-sharp, so to speak. Then you have a brainwave. You contact the editor of the *Widcastle Courier* with a proposition: 'I've got an idea to help with the service your paper offers the community: the town's own 'top 20'. Each week I'll give you a list of the bestselling records in my shop. You can call it your own paper's 'top 20', as long as you just mention each time that the figures are compiled from sales at my shop. Or you can simply call it 'Smith's top 20'.

The editor knows that his readers like a local flavour, and a Widcastle top 20 has more appeal than a national one. What's more, it provides him with free and interesting copy, which is much prized among newspaper editors.

You have to compile your sales figures anyway, so the extra effort is minimal. Having your own top 20 in the paper each week makes your particular shop the official source for the region and gives you an air of authority. The kids are bound to look for that corner of the newspaper each week, and every time they do so the name of Smith's Records is drawn to their attention.

Or if you are a bookseller you could do the same for the top ten fiction and non-fiction books. It won't work for many businesses, of course, but it is surprising how many can do it. For example, you might do a survey or index on 'holiday trends', 'clothing trends' or 'your weekly shopping basket'.

Your own clientele is the first port of call. You already have their names and addresses, you know something about them and you have to send them bills and statements, so there need be no extra postage costs if you send out a questionnaire (except that you will get a better response if you issue reply-paid envelopes).

The top 20 type of index or survey can come from your receipts and figures, while the school-fee type of information can be solicited by sending the clients a simple questionnaire of the box-ticking and 'brief comment' variety.

Whatever results you get from a DIY survey, though, remember that they are only indicators. They might point you in the direction of some urgently needed action. For example, the customers could be quietly dissatisfied with your product or service and have been afraid to say so (a good case for making the replies anonymous). Or the survey might confirm what you already knew. By all means publicise the findings, if there is a message worth telling.

If for any reason you want a proper, scientifically conducted survey, it is a fascinating diversion to work with a competent research organisation and see how they set about discovering what makes people tick. Why do people buy from your rivals down the road? What are the best selling points of your service? What are the worst? You are almost certain to find something you didn't know and which you can put to good use.

But discuss costs first! It can be an expensive operation and most research companies will tailor a survey to some extent according to your means.

There are many companies in this field. Some are listed in the *Yellow Pages*, and your chamber of commerce or trade association may be able to recommend someone. The most comprehensive list is to be found in *The Organisations Book* from: The Market Research Society, 175 Oxford Street, London W1R 1TA (tel 01-439 2585), moving in April 1990 to 15 Northburgh Street, London EC1V 0PR. It is sent free to genuine enquirers.

When you publicise your findings, turn the salient points into a press release, starting with the most eye-catching item and moving quickly to the meat of the story. Keep the press release short and punchy, and send it to the media, with the full survey findings attached for those who want to dig deeper. And, as with all press releases, follow up with phone calls to the journalists concerned.

Chapter 9
Public Speaking

Why Do It?

People tend to treat speaking in public like going to the dentist ... they know it does some good but don't enjoy the experience.

If you think about it, it's crazy to shy away from an opportunity to promote yourself and your business to a captive audience. It wouldn't worry you if half a dozen friends in a pub asked you to tell them about your work, especially if they were thinking of becoming customers. So why baulk at an opportunity to tell perhaps 50 or 100 potential customers?

What salesman could ask for more than to be *invited* by a group of people to tell them, without interruption, about his product for up to half an hour? Speaking in public gives you every businessman's dream — a captive audience.

Here are some reasons for taking public speaking seriously:

☐ It brings you and your company to the notice of a wider public.
☐ It establishes you as an authority in your field.
☐ It makes a contribution to the community of which you and your business are part.
☐ Since communication is a two-way process, it broadens your understanding of the public with whom you expect to do business.
☐ The value of public speaking is the same as that of PR as a whole: it can increase public awareness of your business and products, and help you to put across your point of view.

OK, it takes a certain amount of time and effort, but apart

from that it's free. In fact, in some cases you will even be paid for promoting yourself!

Audience

Finding an audience will usually be the least of your problems. In every town there are rotary clubs, round tables, women's institutes, church societies, schools, colleges, motor clubs, business and professional women's guilds, young farmers' clubs, parent/teacher associations, professional bodies and a host of others. Most of them are crying out for lively speakers on interesting topics.

Surely there are some original and interesting aspects to your business? Say you run a cycle shop. At first it may not sound too exciting, but with a bit of research you could offer talks on: 'The History of the Cycle', 'Road Sense for Young Cyclists', 'The *Tour de France*', 'How to Care for your Bike', and so on. As well as one of these talks interesting non-cyclists in the idea of buying a bicycle, guess where Dad, who was in the audience, will go to buy young Jimmy's bicycle next Christmas?

If you are a baker, farmer, builder, landscape gardener — almost anything — you have the makings of at least one interesting talk. Drop a line to some of the club secretaries and headmasters offering your services and take it from there.

Don't be too upset if sometimes you spend hours rehearsing a speech and turn up to find yourself addressing just half a dozen old dears with broken hearing aids and eyesight which doesn't reach the rostrum, or a handful of bored kids who are being made to listen to you as a punishment for being late for school. Most of the time the audience will be worthwhile. Even if some are small and dreary, word will soon get around if they enjoyed your speech.

Low-key Selling

A public talk is a good sales opportunity, but only if it is kept low-key. All that is required is to interest the audience in bicycle riding and ensure that they know you are Mr Onier of Onier Bikes. You might even get away with an offer for any members of the audience to drop in to the shop for a look at the latest model, but don't take it any further than that.

You won't be thanked for telling them that bicycles are man's greatest invention and that you have got just the thing for them at 10 per cent off for cash purchase. Go into it with the intention of being informative and entertaining, but also modest. And try not to over-expose yourself by speaking at any and every public function. As well as being time-consuming for you, people quickly tire of seeing the same old face all the time.

Preparation of Speech

Who are my audience?

The Widcastle Retired Rat Catchers Association has asked you to give them a talk and you have accepted. Now what? Unless you are one of those incredible people who can scribble down a few notes just beforehand and give a scintillating speech, most of the success on the day lies in thorough preparation.

The first task is to ask your host a few things about the audience:

☐ Roughly how many?
☐ What ages?
☐ What backgrounds and interests?
☐ Will they have been eating/drinking, or will they have their tongues hanging out waiting for you to finish?
☐ What subjects and type of speech are they used to?

Some speakers will also ask if it is an all-male audience so that they can tell a few dirty stories to warm them up. If dirty stories are your forte then you may land a few extra laughs, but it is rather sad if you have to depend on them to compensate for an inability to hold the audience any other way.

How long?

While asking your host about the audience, find out about the facilities, such as a rostrum, amplification etc (see the section on 'knowing your ground', pages 149-51) and ask how long they want you to speak for. Most of these talks are expected to last for about 20 to 30 minutes. Be *very* wary of speaking for longer. Only a gifted few can hold an audience for more than half an hour.

Unless you have a lot of important material to communicate, or if they are really insistent on a long speech, it is enough to talk for 20 minutes or even less. However, if you have some

143

good slides or film you can keep the audience involved for longer. Conversely, if asked to give an impromptu after-dinner speech, don't for God's sake go on for more than two or three minutes.

One way of judging how much to prepare is to read aloud, fairly slowly, a passage from a book or newspaper for one minute. Then count the number of words, and multiply by the number of minutes you are to speak for. This will give you a rough idea of how many words to write.

Writing the Speech

Now it is time to prepare what you are going to say. Some people like to write a speech down word-for-word, while others rely on headings. No particular method is compulsory. Try it different ways and see which suits you best, though I confess to being an inveterate writer of the entire script.

Start with a 'framework'. What are the main points you want to get over? Jot them down as you think of them, then put them into a logical order so that there is some flow, thus:

The Pleasures of Cycling	
Main points	*Sub-points*
Health and fitness	Quote from article in paper about:
Enjoy scenery	increase in cyclists . . .
What does it cost?	Kid who couldn't ride . . .
Maintenance: importance; how to do it	
Road safety	
Low cost of cycling	
Teaching youngsters	
Cycle racing	
Riding hints: height of saddle; handlebars, position of feet etc	

These are then put in order. If traffic jams have been in the news lately you might start by talking about what is uppermost in their minds:

Main points	*Sub-points*
Faster by bike	
Low cost of cycling	Quote from article in paper
	How much it costs
Health and fitness	Mention cycle racing
No pollution	
Enjoy scenery	

Riding hints	Height of saddle etc
Maintenance and tips	
Road safety	
Teaching youngsters	Joke: kid who couldn't ride

What you now have is the makings of something which can grab their attention at the start and then take them through the basics of cycling stage by stage.

You can start by hitting them with the realities of running a car and, having heard a *good* gag about a garage offering a free car with every hundred gallons or something, fit it into the text.

This leads you naturally into some favourable statistics about the money you can save by cycling instead of driving. The point is reinforced by quoting a short cutting from the local paper on the subject. Note that one of the original main points (of which there were too many) has become a 'sub-point' and you just give them a brief idea. Otherwise you will spend half the time going on about money.

This speech is about the *pleasures* of cycling, so you can now move from the cost advantages to how cycling can make you stay young, ward off heart disease and lose weight. It was turning into a long speech, so you cut cycle racing as a whole topic and give it just a mention at this stage. Then you move on to stressing how much more you can enjoy the scenery from a bike, and so on.

Keep the sentences short and simple. Try to picture yourself actually saying the words on the night.

Jokes

For some reason people assume that you haven't made a speech until you have tried to emulate the worst stand-up comic. Jokes are *not* compulsory and, unless they are genuinely funny, are a disadvantage. They can detract from your main message, and if they fall flat it is a question of who is most embarrassed — you or the audience. One gag that they have all heard can undo hours of hard work on the speech.

However, if you know some relevant jokes which you are sure the audience will enjoy, and if you are certain that you can tell them well, they can certainly improve their enjoyment of the speech. In short, jokes are fine so long as they work, but if in doubt stay off them. Why not see, instead, if you can come up with some original humorous comments? The cutting from the paper might have mentioned, for example, that the Mayor of Widcastle now rides to work on a bike, at which point you could make an aside like: 'It's the same as any other bike, except that it has a gold chain.'

Best of all are humorous anecdotes. If you can get your message over with a few amusing episodes drawn from life, you will find people listening. It's the same principle as the television interviews: people love stories. Likewise, the serious messages can be got over with serious stories rather than a lot of finger-wagging and tub-thumping.

Plugs

In a way, this speech on cycling is one long plug for your product. Some speeches may be less obvious and will need the introduction of a few plugs. But remember that it is a low-key sales pitch, so any plugs should be few and subtle.

Why should they be interested?

Always remember when writing a speech that what interests *you* does not necessarily interest *them*. If you watch any group of people on a public speaking course you will find that the ones who are most confident beforehand (assuming equal degrees of previous experience) are usually those who are talking about a familiar subject — their job, their hobby, golf, motor racing. They are also the most consistently boring.

While you write the speech, keep asking yourself: 'Why should this be of the least interest to them?' Put yourself in their shoes. You love bicycles and can't believe that the whole world doesn't love them too. But, if you assume from the start that your audience can't bear the things, you will give a much more interesting speech. It is the difference between boring them with 'It takes half an hour to cycle into town from here . . .' and getting their minds working with 'No doubt you've seen people cycling into town and wondered why they didn't get the bus . . .'

Use of language

(No, you fool, not *that* sort of language!) With public speaking the same principles of brevity and simplicity apply as for all communication — only more so. When someone is reading something at least he has the chance of an action replay if there is a bit he doesn't understand. He can go back and read it through again. But with a speech the audience has to get it first time.

Also, the listener's brain is bombarded with word after word, statement after statement, fact after fact. So it is very important to keep your sentences short, sharp and simple. If you write the speech out in full, try if possible to use a type-writer with a large typeface and leave a good space between sentences. Keep the paragraphs very short and leave plenty of air between them. That way you will tend to pause between statements, which is important if each pearl of wisdom is to sink in properly. It also makes it easier for you to find your place if you get lost.

Many good speakers mark their scripts to remind them where to stress particular words and when to pause for effect.

Try reading this to an audience in a hurry: 'Have you ever tried riding a bicycle through the streets of this town? If you do, you're in for a shock!'

You could stress almost any word or combination of words in the first sentence and change the emphasis. This is off-putting for you as a speaker because your brain is frantically asking: 'Quick, where do I put the emphasis in this one?' A 30-minute speech has 4000 to 5000 words in it, which means an awful lot of quick subconscious decisions.

Without something to remind you to pause after that first question it is easy to gabble on into the next point before the first one has sunk in. It helps to mark the speech in advance, thus:

'Have *you* ever tried riding a bicycle through the streets of this town? If you *do* you're in for a shock!'

The need to summarise

The old adage about a speech having a beginning, a middle and an end is a good one. You should make them know you have begun by starting with a bang, hold their attention with the 'meat' of the speech, and then make sure they know you have finished.

A useful approach is to drum home your main points near the beginning, and again at the end in a 'summary' form. Having got them listening to the low cost of cycling, you could say: 'So for the next few minutes, let us look at cycling. We'll see how it can save you money, improve your health ...' and so on for the rest of your main points. At the end you can spend a few seconds winding up with a reminder of what you have told them.

Notes

Having written or thought out what you want to say, there is the question of how you are going to present it. Some speakers try to memorise the lot or just rely on a few 'bullet points' on a card. Some transfer the headlines on to postcards, while others prefer a great sheaf of papers with the full speech typed out.

There are no hard and fast rules and you can be sceptical of those who swear by one method or the other. Some argue that lots of paper is distracting. There is also a school of thought that says you look more polished if you don't rely on notes at all (true, until you forget your lines). The main thing is to find which system suits *you*.

Notes are, after all, supposed to be an aid. They are there to help you, so use them to help you make a better speech. The important thing is not to read from them or you will have the whole audience snoring inside five minutes. Hence the importance of spacing sentences and paragraphs well out so that you can easily look down and find your place when you need a prompt. If you use cards stick to one-line notes, again well spread out.

'you will have the whole audience snoring inside five minutes'

Practice

The best way to avoid over-reliance on notes is to have practised the speech several times in advance. Read it through a few times first, then try reading it aloud into a tape recorder. This is particularly valuable as it picks up awkward expressions and tongue twisters in plenty of time for you to make alterations. It also gives you a true indication of the length of the speech.

Preparation: 'Knowing Your Ground'

Nothing is more off-putting than to walk into a strange hall full of strange people. You can avoid much anguish by knowing your ground. So, shortly before the speech, go along to the hall and have a look round. What is the seating like? Will they be packed in tight or spread out? Will they be comfortable or likely to fidget because of hard chairs? Can they see you?

What are the acoustics like? Will they be able to hear you or will you need amplification. If so, get your hosts to organise it. Then check that it works and that the microphone is at the right height. Very importantly, will you be using a lectern? (We will look at the advantages and disadvantages of this later.) If there is no lectern, or you don't want one, what height is the table? Is it high enough to read your notes from or will you need to hold them? Or will you just stand there with no 'protection' from a table or lectern?

All these are important points. They can make the difference between a memorable performance and a shambles. You won't get many new converts to cycling if they can't hear you, can't see you, or if they are suffering from cramp and you can't see your notes.

Visual aids

If you are going to use any sort of visual aids it is essential to check that they are functioning first. Have at least one dry run beforehand.

It is not enough simply to ask the hosts to lay on a 'projector'. Do you mean a cine or slide projector? If cine, is it 35, 16 or 8 millimetre? With or without sound? If slide, do you want a 'Carousel' or some other type? How big is the screen and how long is the 'throw'? Do you need a skilled projectionist? Has the equipment got the right plugs? Is the lead long enough? Have you got a spare bulb?

149

With any type of visual aid always ask: 'Will they all be able to see it?' It is not a stupid question. Many presentations are ruined by half the audience having to peer hard at illegible pictures and letters, and then giving up and talking among themselves.

I have seen a very senior official of a large organisation turn up 'cold' to give a speech which depended entirely on 'word slides'. The screen was too small, the projector too close and there were too many words and figures on the slides (including the entire organisation chart of a nationalised industry on one 35mm slide, a masterpiece of photographic skill but totally unreadable).

Different speakers use visual aids in different ways, ranging from all pictures and no talk to all talk and no pictures. Again, it's up to you to find what suits you best, but as a general rule remember that they are visual *aids*. The most important thing is what you have to tell the audience. Slides, films and flip charts are only there to help you get the message over.

If you say in your speech 'The ultimate in bike riding is the *Tour de France*' and accompany it with a slide showing the words 'The ultimate in bike riding is the *Tour de France*' (don't laugh, people do that sort of thing all the time), you are not achieving very much. If, however, the statement is accompanied by a colourful slide of hundreds of cycle racers hurtling down a hill in the *Tour de France* you are illustrating your talk effectively.

There are plenty of people to approach for help with visual aids. You can try:

☐ *Yellow Pages* ('Audio Visual Equipment', 'Film Producers' etc)
☐ Audio and video trade magazines (notably *Audio Visual*).
☐ Local chamber of commerce.
☐ PR or marketing departments of big local firms who use AV advertising agencies.
☐ PR consultants.
☐ Your own trade association.
☐ Business organisations: CBI, Industrial Society, BIM etc.
☐ Local university, trade schools etc.
☐ Conference organisers.

There is a full explanation of how to use them in the chapter on 'Audio Visual' in *Employee Communications in the 1980s.**

* Michael Bland (1980) *Employee Communications in the 1980s* Kogan Page: London

Very briefly, the main methods available are:

1. *Chalkboard.* The disadvantage is that it is difficult to talk and write at the same time. You must turn round frequently to face the audience.
2. *Flip charts.* Useful. Cheap and easy to prepare. Can't be seen by big audience.
3. *Overhead projector.* You can make your own 'slides' cheaply and project the picture behind you while facing the audience.
4. *Slides.* The most common and versatile medium. Can range from a single projector to multiple projection with 'cross fade', animation and several pictures on the screen. But keep it simple.
5. *Film strip.* Small and light. Disadvantage is that you can't alter individual pictures once the strip is made.
6. *Film.* Short clips of film to illustrate a point can make a useful break in the speech. Wakes people up and gives you a breather. Equipment and cost can be problems.
7. *Video.* Good for keeping audience interested. But beware of showing a good video before or during your speech as you will seem very flat after the video. Show it at the end if possible.

Having prepared the speech and visual aids, checked the location and rehearsed, you are ready to go. The first thing that hits most speakers, however small and friendly the occasion, is NERVES.

Nerves

This can vary from a slight tingling in the stomach to violent palpitations. It can sometimes cause you to dry up completely. There is no instant remedy, but one consolation is the fact that almost everybody — experienced speakers and even actors and television personalities — suffer from nerves before making a speech.

In addition to the tips in Chapter 4, it is useful to remember that even though you feel as though you are crumbling away inside, even though your hands are shaking, your voice quavering and heart pounding . . . *the audience doesn't notice it nearly as much as you think.* Moreover, the nerves will almost certainly start to disappear once you get going.

The single best way to reduce the effect of nerves is to

prepare the speech thoroughly so that you don't suddenly dry up with a hundred pairs of eyes fixed on you. Ask for a glass of water to be handy, too, so that you can avoid getting hoarse.

The one thing not to do is to try to kill your pre-speech nerves with alcohol. The mixture of booze and tension can cause havoc. Sometimes a single dose of spirits can help, but avoid it if you can.

Stance

One delightful book on public speaking tells you to 'stand with your feet 400 millimetres apart'. If you haven't a micrometer handy just stand upright and relaxed, with your feet slightly apart.

Try to stay in the same place as much as you can, without appearing 'rooted'. There is no harm in moving occasionally but if you do so, do it boldly and firmly. Don't shuffle, sway or pace up and down.

Then there are your hands. In everyday life — talking to colleagues, at meetings, waiting at a bus stop — you don't notice your hands, yet the moment you start to speak to an audience your hands become the most embarrassing thing about you. Speakers stuff them deep in their pockets, clasp them behind their backs or hold on to the rostrum for dear life with them.

Try not to worry about them. If you want to put them out of the way you can hold them, fingers touching, at stomach level, but don't be afraid to use them. It adds life if you occasionally hold out your hands to stress something, or point a finger at the audience.

Likewise, don't be embarrassed by your notes or note cards. If you have a lectern on which to keep notes out of sight, so much the better. But if not, don't try to hide them or fidget with them nervously. The audience won't be offended that you are using them, so hold them up and be proud of them.

It is possible nowadays to hire an Autocue conference screen. This is a small glass panel on top of the lectern which looks like clear glass to the audience but which rolls your notes for you, as if you were a newsreader. You are happily reading your speech while the audience thinks you are looking at them. It's OK for the professional, but much misused by the inexperienced. It is also expensive to hire and requires a skilled operator.

Most speeches are given from behind a lectern. This has the

double advantage of giving you somewhere to put your notes and acting as a shield. You can hide most of your body behind it.

A lectern, however, is a double-edged weapon. If the audience can only see a head and shoulders entrenched behind the lectern it is much less interesting than seeing the whole of a speaker, especially if he or she moves around a bit and uses plenty of hand signals. Also, if you get used to speaking only from a lectern it can be terrifying when you find yourself having to make a speech without one. You suddenly feel as if you have forgotten your trousers.

It is worth practising speeches with and without a lectern, so that you are equally at home either way.

Eye contact

Do you remember how you learnt most from those school-teachers who always appeared to be looking at *you* personally, so you didn't dare not to pay attention? Eye contact is a good way of keeping an audience on its toes.

It is really quite simple. Glance at your notes only when you have to. The rest of the time your eyes should look at the audience, fixing different areas for a few seconds at a time. Because they are not too close to you, each member of the audience feels that you are looking straight at him or her, when in fact your eyes are taking in a cluster of half a dozen people.

At the same time avoid staring any individual straight in the eye. The return gaze can make you feel self-conscious and put you off your stride.

In the words you use and the way you look at the audience, pretend that you are only addressing yourself to one person, as though each individual member of the audience is the most important one there.

Voice

Voice projection is important. You want each person to hear you, but without shouting. When checking the hall out before-hand get someone to sit at the back and make sure they can hear you. Then allow for the fact that on the night there will be a certain amount of coughing and shuffling to compete with.

Pretend that at the back of the hall is a slightly deaf aunt. Speak up and speak clearly. Pronounce the words clearly and talk at a slightly slower pace than usual.

If using a microphone, make sure that it is at the right height and position — a foot or so in front of you and at about neck level. Practise speaking into it because used wrongly it can do more harm than good. If you are too close you can get a 'feedback' howl from the amplifiers, and if you stand too far back or wander away from the microphone your words will be lost completely.

Don't be afraid of pauses. If you dry up or lose your place, a couple of seconds can seem like an eternity, but it doesn't seem that way to the audience. Stop for a few seconds from time to time. It lets the words sink in and wakes the audience up. They think: 'he's stopped . . . what's he going to say next?' Far from sharing your embarrassment they actually get quite excited to see what's coming.

After the Speech

With the speech successfully finished, all that is left is to breathe a sigh of relief and enjoy whatever food and drinks may have been laid on.

Sometimes there are 'panel' sessions. The only thing to avoid is the temptation to waffle, as a panel is probably the only time that anybody asks for your opinion and then lets you finish what you have to say.

People are bound to come up afterwards and congratulate you on a marvellous speech, but don't let it go to your head. There is no relationship between the congratulations and the quality of the speech. Probably the biggest single contributor to the world's interminable bores is the vote of thanks by which someone who has just made a speech of soporific length and abysmal quality is heartily congratulated on his informative and entertaining talk. Aglow with praise, the speaker goes on to accept more speaking engagements and offer speeches of even greater length and less significance.

If you *really* want to know how you did, get your husband or wife to sit through the speech and give you an honest opinion afterwards. Another indication of a good speech is when people from the audience come up afterwards and ask you to speak to some other organisation. If they are prepared to go through it again it can't have been that bad.

Press

Remember the point in Chapter 3 about using a speech as a peg for a press release. If you have an important point to make, and you have cleared it with your hosts beforehand, you can use 'speaking to members of the Widcastle Destitutes' Society today . . .' as an excuse for a one-pager to the local press.

If you have the facilities, send copies of the whole speech to the press so that they can look for any other item of interest, but always accompany the full text with the press release. If they have to plough through 30 pages of script to find the key argument you won't get much coverage.

Make sure that both the press release and the script say *what* the occasion is, *when* and *where*, *who* is speaking, and the *subject*. Embargo the speech until the time you are actually making it, and type at least once on each page the words 'Please check against delivery'. This means that if you omit anything, or change what you say, the onus is on the press to get it right. It does not mean, however, that they *cannot* publish what you have written if you say something different on the night.

Public Speaking Checklist

---

1. Audience: how many, ages, background and interests etc.
2. Facilities: rostrum, amplification etc.
3. Length of speech.
4. Speech:
   - ☐ Write down points to make, plus jokes and other comments and put into logical order.
   - ☐ Start with something topical or 'grabbing'.
   - ☐ Jokes can help but are not vital.
   - ☐ Include some low-key plugs for your company or product.
   - ☐ Look for ways of making your material interesting to them.
   - ☐ Wind up with a brief summary.
   - ☐ Keep the sentences short and simple.
   - ☐ Underline words to be sressed.
5. Rehearse the speech.
6. Check the hall beforehand for seating, acoustics, lectern.
7. Visual aids:
   - ☐ Be specific about equipment.
   - ☐ Have a 'dry run' and make sure it works.

8. Delivery:
   ☐ You don't look as nervous as you feel.
   ☐ Don't move around too much, but don't be 'rooted'.
   ☐ Try not to be conscious of your hands, or your notes.
   ☐ Maintain eye contact.
   ☐ Speak clearly, and check microphone if used.

Chapter 10
Being a Good Neighbour

What It Means

Sc me businesses go to great lengths to be responsible members
cf the community. Others don't give a damn. But whatever the
argument about their value to the business, community relations
are an important part of public relations.

Community relations can cover almost anything from giving
a prize to the local hospital's best student nurse to donating a
cheque to the RSPCA. Whether you sponsor a fund-raising
event, show a bunch of screaming kids round your premises or
pay for the production of the *Widcastle Town Guide*, it is all
community relations. It's about your business being a good
neighbour and, some would argue, being *seen* to be a good
neighbour.

Why Bother?

Audiences

Most of the audiences at whom your public relations are aimed —
journalists, financiers, authorities, customers — are also
members of the local community. The bank manager from
whom you are trying to borrow money or the client to whom
you are hoping to sell a big order may also be the treasurer of
the local NSPCC branch or a governor of the Widcastle High
School.

At the very least they probably read the newspapers which
report the fortunes of these organisations. Although it is a very
scattered form of target hitting, community relations is yet
another way of getting at your various audiences.

Association of name

It is also another way of getting people to hear your name. One of the aims of public relations is for people to have heard of you through channels other than advertising. The award of the 'Fred Smith Trophy' or an expression of gratitude by the mothers' union for your contribution of half a ton of marmalade are examples of how the public can get to hear of you.

Warm glow

Most importantly, community relations can give people a good feeling about you. All too often business is seen in an unfavourable light. To many people 'business' means noisy factories, exploitation of labour and parasitical profits. So, it doesn't do any harm to have your company associated in the public mind with good causes.

Just because . . .

There is still such a thing as good old-fashioned altruism. For all the spiteful things that are said about them, there are many businessmen who contribute to the community simply because they want to. Some do so in secret, on the grounds that if you publicise it it's not really charity, while others give for the right reasons but grab a bit of kudos while they are at it. Either way, one benefit is that it can give *you* a good feeling, too.

Disadvantages of a 'Good Neighbour' Policy

Compared with other forms of PR, community relations has some disadvantages.

Not direct

Whereas you can tailor, say, a speech or a press release to aim at particular target groups, a community relations exercise is much more random in its audience appeal. You can also relate PR more directly to your product or service and treat it as a form of free advertising, but with community relations it is usually only your name that is publicised.

There are exceptions. Obviously if you run a furniture store and donate half a dozen armchairs to the old folk's home, you are getting some product association too.

Cost effectiveness

For PR generally it is difficult to prove that there is a 'bottom line'. Unlike money spent on manufacturing or selling, you can't prove that PR gives any immediate benefits. This is even more the case with community relations. There are many arguments for it being worthwhile, but the value of community relations cannot be added up on the profit and loss statements.

Limited advertising

If you do something to help the community you can't do too much shouting about it or people will suspect your motives. Of course, each activity buys goodwill from the individual group which is benefiting, and it can also lead to public acknowledgements, or mentions in the *Widcastle Courier*, but if your sole motive is publicity it is an expensive way of setting about it.

Sometimes it is possible to do both — to give and to receive. If, for example, you were to donate a minibus to a children's home no one would think any worse of you if the minibus were to have your company's name plastered all over it. But again it's a very pricey form of advertising.

Bottomless pit

And if you donate a minibus with your name on it, you can guarantee a score of appeals every week from various worthy causes asking if they can have one too. One act of generosity goes round the other hopeful charities like wildfire.

If you go in for being a good neighbour you will end up having to play God. You can only afford to become involved with a certain number of projects, to present so many trophies and hand over a certain number of cheques. Yet there are hundreds of thousands of deserving causes — schools, playgroups, sports clubs, hospitals, and a vast host of other organisations which do good things and need your help. The more you do, the more you find yourself having to say 'no'.

Is It Worth It?

On balance, the advantages of community relations outweigh the disadvantages, particularly if you set about it in the right way. Often a few minutes of thought are worth far more than a fat cheque. There are, alas, one or two companies which believe that giving a big chunk of money to the Scouts or PTA will buy off the local community and stop them complaining about the noxious fumes or unbearable noise. But the answer lies, not in the amount of *money* you contribute, but in the amount of *thought*.

Almost every business has something with which it can help the community. More often than not, all that is needed is the loan of an empty warehouse for the choir to practice, the donation of some unwanted meat to the dogs' home or the temporary allocation of a couple of second-hand cars from your forecourt to the local road safety training scheme.

The list of things you can do for the local community is almost endless, but below are some ideas for how you can be a good neighbour without breaking the bank. Most are examples of the community relations activities of various real companies.

Prizes

Raffles and tombolas are probably the most popular form of fund raising, as anyone who has been lumbered with a book of tickets to sell will know. The prizes for these raffles come from all sorts of sources: some are bought by the fund raisers, some are unwanted gifts or donated by generous members of the public, and some are given by companies.

Maybe you are in the business where you can donate something which you make or sell yourself, some obvious examples being wine merchants, food stores, clothiers, manufacturers of luxury goods, television retailers etc. If you are not in that line of work then you might be able to buy something appropriate or present one of your normal promotional handouts.

Sometimes there is the added bonus of a grateful acknowledgement being added to the raffle tickets or programme of events, but in any case the charity organisers will appreciate what you have done.

Another possibility is a trophy for winning the school sack race or for the nurse who empties the most bedpans. Colleges, schools, clubs and so on always want incentives for their members and students. You might find that the police are running a road safety quiz contest among the local schools. If the contest is for the 'Bloggs' Bakery Cup' Mr Bloggs will have bought a lot of goodwill among the police and the schools for his few pounds.

Charity advertising

Fetes, carnivals, open days and other public gatherings often involve a souvenir programme in which companies buy 'space'. The deal is that the company gets some publicity while the organisers get the money. While your ad may only be seen by a few hundred people (and a certain amount of money which could have gone straight to charity is lost in paying for the artwork block) it can be a sensible system for contributing, and at the same time receiving some sort of public acknowledgement.

Sponsorships

Companies are forever being asked to sponsor things. Kids go for walks or compete in spelling-bees to raise money for the mentally handicapped. Netball teams ask for sponsorship to keep them supplied with nets and balls, while the occasional lunatic walks round the world pushing a wheelbarrow with a square wheel at 10 pence a mile for the Home for Distressed Vegetarians.

At the top of the scale there is a substantial industry in sponsorship of the arts and of sport, with some big firms (notably the tobacco companies whose advertising is restricted) spending millions of pounds on football clubs, golf tournaments, test matches and concerts.

These principles can also be applied locally, though it can still be an expensive operation to fund a tennis tournament or piano recital. The appeals from the organisers will always offer not-to-be-missed publicity, but only very rarely will sponsorship be as effective as direct advertising.

There are exceptions, such as a car dealer sponsoring the local motor club rally or a sports shop sponsoring the football team, where there is a close relationship between the product and the particular event. However, most sponsorships are little more than a charitable handout, which may have plenty of merit in its own right.

Goods and services

There are probably scores of needy organisations in your neighbourhood which you could help from your business without much sacrifice. For example, engineering companies of all sizes often make or adapt equipment for the handicapped,

'the occasional
lunatic walks
round the world
pushing a
wheelbarrow with
a square wheel'

or you might find a building company using its minibus at the weekend to take deprived children to the seaside.

Is there room in your shop window for advertisements for the town show or a fund-raising activity? If you are an electrician or carpenter could the church do with some expert help with its wiring or with the repair of broken pews? Is there any way in which *your* product or experience could be used to help someone? It doesn't always have to be free. You have to make a living, but often all that is wanted is a discount, or some cheap 'seconds'.

Similarly, the experience you have acquired over the years in building up your business might save somebody else a great deal of time and money. For example, in many towns there are schemes for helping the unemployed to learn new skills. By offering some expert training you can help the community, and might also be lining up some future trained employees.

Education

There are dozens of ways to make a good name for yourself in the local schools and colleges. As well as giving them much needed help, you are getting through to future customers (and employees) in a low-key way.

Again, you might be able to help with unwanted materials which have very little resale value for you. Primary schools and art departments, for instance, are always scavenging for off-cuts such as pieces of leather, cloth, wood and paper. Craft departments need engines, lathes, drills, screws and equipment. If you use any sort of posters, wall charts or service charts they might be just what one of the classes is looking for.

It may be, too, that the pupils would benefit from a talk by you on careers or some aspect of your business. If you run any kind of factory or manufacturing process it is almost certain that some of the teachers would like to bring their class round for an educational visit.

You may be able to help with useful handouts. Just one example is the 'glow worm'. This is a reflecting disc at the end of a length of cotton which the kids can pin to their clothes so that car headlights pick them up when the children are walking home from school on dark winter evenings. A local businessman could supply all the primary school children in his small town with 'glow worms' for just a few hundred pounds. That's a lot of community relations for a small amount. It is also an act which would certainly make a story in the local press if you wanted to get some publicity for your public spirited gesture.

Charitable contributions

You have seen it many times. The philanthropic businessman and the grateful charity organiser smile meaningfully into the camera and hold up the cheque, which is another contribution to the businessman's 'knighthood fund'.

Whether you contribute to charities or not (either from your own pocket or that of your business) is your personal decision and you don't need a book to tell you if you should do it. If you give, the opportunities are there to get some coverage. But is it really charity if you do it for the publicity?

To some extent the same question applies to all the good works mentioned in this chapter. Are you doing it to help someone or to show what a caring company you have? Or is it a bit of both? It would seem more legitimate to publicise some activities (for example, sponsoring of a local 'paraplegic olympics') than others (cash donation to a national charity). In the final analysis, it is really a matter for your own judgement and conscience.

Chapter 11
From Ministers to Mickey Mouse

We have looked at the main methods of promoting yourself and getting messages over. There are many others. This last chapter is a collection of different PR activities. The list is far from comprehensive. You could start publicising your company today and still be coming up with new ideas when you retire.

Perhaps some of the following items could have had a chapter of their own (government relations and internal communications, for example), but not many small businessmen will want to indulge in redrafting 'green papers' or establishing employee communication networks.

All this chapter aims to do is to show some of the many different types of audience and PR methods which can be added to your 'armoury'.

Government Authorities

Parliament, Whitehall and local authorities can be important 'audiences' because, unlike the rest of us, they have the power to change things. You may need to get through to them for one of two reasons:

- ☐ To change something which affects you (proposal to build a motorway through your shop; compulsory levies; even the law itself).
- ☐ To get something done to your benefit (planning approval, government grants etc).

These 'audiences' will only rarely be approached for the reasons of positive publicity (ie attempts to boost sales) that this book is mainly about. Occasionally you might, for example, lobby your MP and publicise the fact in your local paper. Or there is the classic example of presenting some authority or other with a petition, but mostly it is a matter of making a direct approach for a specific purpose.

In a sense, then, dealing with governments and authorities can be more of a business activity and less of a PR-type drive to sell more products. But they can often be essential to survival itself, and the right sort of approach is important.

Moreover, there are ways in which your MP or town councillor can be a target for your 'warm glow' publicity. For instance, you may have made it known to the general public that you have been a good neighbour by planting a screen of trees in front of the factory. Then why not make sure the Environmental Health Department, too, knows how good you have been, not to mention getting it home to that fool on the council who keeps making your life a misery.

Let us take a very brief, general look at some of the ways of approaching the right people and organisations. In specific cases you will probably be able to get help from your trade association or representative body, and in many cases the simplest thing is to ask direct. If you want to draw up a petition to Parliament in the correct fashion, for example, you can ask the Petitions Office at the House of Commons for advice. Government departments and local authorities have information departments who will tell you how to set about a particular approach.

Members of Parliament

Despite all the flak they get, most MPs do a lot of beavering behind the scenes for constituents with problems. If you are the victim of some unfairness — from VAT harassment to having your rhubarb crop ruined by the shadow from a new factory block — it may well be worth asking your MP to take up cudgels on your behalf.

Often he or she can get results with little more than a well worded letter on impressive looking paper with a portcullis embossed on it. And an MP has more high-level contacts in appropriate places than a small business person.

If it really comes to the crunch he has the ability to 'ask questions' on your behalf. This may take the form of a direct approach to the ministry responsible for your difficulty, or he may even ask a question in the House. By now you are getting a public airing and causing a certain amount of bureaucratic squirming. Sometimes these questions make their way into the national newspapers, but usually the only written publicity will be the local press (your job to publicise, after clearing it with the MP) and the ledgers of *Hansard*.

'well worth asking your MP to take up cudgels on your behalf'

Ultimately an MP can change the law itself if the case is big enough, either by contributing to the parliamentary debate on a proposed law or by drafting and proposing a Private Member's Bill.

If you don't know who your MP is, you should. He or she will appear regularly for one reason or another in the local press, and many advertise their 'surgeries' in the local paper.

An MP can be contacted by attending one of these 'surgeries' or by writing to him by name ('Mr Fred Smith, MP') at the House of Commons, London SW1A 0AA. If it is urgent you can ring the House on 01-219 3000 and ask for the particular MP. As they are usually tied up in debates or other business you can be put through to the 'Members' answering service' and ask to be rung back. Remember that they are genuinely busy people and may not always have time to do so.

Despite the workload an MP will usually respond to an invitation to visit your premises and get to know you. If your business is a corner newsagent's or one-man plumbing service it is perhaps unfair to expect a visit. But if you employ people, make things or provide valuable services, you are an important constituent.

Instead of waiting for a crisis send an open invitation for him or her to come and learn about your business, your problems and what you do for the community.

You may even be able to get some joint publicity. It is in a Member's interest to stay in the public eye; hence the pictures that appear so frequently in the local press of some honourable friend operating a lathe or kneading the dough. One newspaper recently showed an MP delivering milk at 6.00 am — a nice piece of promotion for both the MP and the dairy concerned.

With his permission, send a press release and photograph to the local media, and if the event is different enough invite the local TV and radio.

Euro MPs

If your business has any kind of EEC involvement you could find your Euro MP useful. You may export or import to the Common Market, in which case you will be affected by EEC legislation and trading policies. Even if you think you have no connection whatsoever, you might suddenly find your business being loused up by some obscure European directive on lawnmower noise, quality of bathing water, the grading of cauliflowers or the contents of a loaf of bread (all genuine examples).

MEPs (Members of the European Parliament) do not have as much power as their national counterparts. The European Parliament has a fair bit of *influence* on the wondrous workings of the EEC but it does not actually make the laws. However, an MEP can help you in many ways. If you want to expand your business into European markets, for example, he or she can give you advice based on experience of the intricate machinations of the EEC. If the latest draft proposal on the width of left-handed tea mug handles is going to affect your production of leftimugs, your MEP is the first point of contact.

The MEP's constituency is much bigger than that of an MP, but you should still get a response from an invitation to visit if your business has any sort of European angle. Very few of them hold 'surgeries' but you can contact an MEP by writing to him or her at:

European Community Commission
8 Storey's Gate
London SW1P 3AT.

You can find out the name of your MEP from the Information Office.

Government departments

Whitehall is the nation's real centre of power. While Parliament is like the board of directors which decides on general policy, the Civil Service is the executive management which actually does things. Often the answer to a problem, be it a grant to develop a new factory or competition from rogue imports, lies in some far corner of SW1.

There is no PR mileage to be gained from your dealings with these people. It only gets their backs up. But it is still worth knowing how to approach them when the need arises.

The first thing to remember is that the much-maligned 'them' are in fact real people, most of them very competent and surprisingly approachable. Finding the right one is the biggest problem. For each problem there is a particular ministry with a particular division with a particular office and a particular person who can help with your problem.

Instead of exchanging endless letters, pick up the telephone, ask directory enquiries for the phone number of the ministry you want (if you live in London they are in the directory), ring them and ask to speak to the information office. Explain the problem and they will usually give you an appropriate name and extension number, or put you through to the right ministry. It can make all the difference in the world when you actually have a fellow human being to discuss things with.

It doesn't always work. Some civil servants still believe that they are not allowed to divulge their names (which is rubbish and should be taken up with your MP if it happens), and of course there is no guarantee that you will be awarded that grant or relieved from having to fill in that 70-page survey form, but the chances will be much better if you discuss it personally with a civil servant who knows the score.

If the direct approach fails, and you still believe you have a case, it is time to write to:

Department of Employment
Small Firms Division
Steel House
Tothill Street
London SW1H 9NF
Freefone Enterprise reached through dialling 100.

Local authorities

These can be quite a hotch-potch. You may have four different problems and find that one is the responsibility of the district council, one of the county council, one of the borough council and one the parish council. Nevertheless, once you have identified whose province the problem is in, the principle of direct contact still applies. Almost all authorities and Town Halls have press or information offices who can set you off in the right direction.

To describe the workings of these authorities in a few sentences would be like trying to summarise the Bible on one side of A4. For example, if you have a problem of access to your premises which is caused by the conditon of the road or traffic congestion, you may find that various parts of the responsibility lie with the county council, the police and two or three different departments of the borough council.

This is where your local councillor can be a big help. Like an MP, he or she is someone who, as you are an employer and business person, you should get to know as soon as possible. Often a councillor will be able to guide you through the labyrinth of local government, take up your case at council meetings or point you in the right direction if the problem is outside his area. Again like MPs, councillors often benefit from publicity, so you may be able to work jointly on a press release.

Most cases will be the province of a borough or town councillor, who can be found via the information office of the local town hall, or adverts for 'surgeries' in the local press.

Always bear in mind that these various authorities, from government departments to parish councils, are among your important 'audiences'. Instead of going to them only when there is a crisis, keep them abreast of developments in your business and remind them occasionally of your existence.

They won't thank you for flooding them with weekly missives, but whenever there is a development like a new factory or product, more or less jobs or a big new contract, send a copy of the press release or appropriate literature to the relevant contacts, such as your MP, councillor and government and local authorities.

Representative Bodies

Another route to the various authorities is via a trade association or representative body. Almost every occupation has its own federation or association and there are dozens of more general ones such as the Confederation of British Industry (which has a Small Firms Council), the Institute of Directors (which any company director can join), the local Chamber of Commerce (and/or the Association of British Chambers of Commerce), the Association of Independent Businesses, and so on.

There are so many organisations doing so many things to help the small business person that a guide called *Which Voice?* is available from:

Leicestershire Small Firms Centre
8 St Martins,
Leicester LE1 5DD.

Probably the most active campaigner on the small business person's behalf is:

National Federation of Self Employed and Small Businesses
32 St Annes Road West
Lytham St Annes
Lancashire FY8 1NY.

These representative bodies are valuable for much more than just taking up your case with the appropriate authorities. They can offer advice on tax and VAT, company law, employment problems etc.

The NFSESB even runs weekend PR courses where its members can learn the principles of active public relations and practise writing press releases, speaking in public and being interviewed on radio and television. Another invaluable service is the National Federation's 'An Inspector at the Door', which is a guide to Britain's army of different inspectors — from hygiene to horticulture — and tells you what rights they do or don't have.

Joining a representative body and taking part in its proceedings can be a useful extension to your general PR and can also provide a forum for swapping business ideas and getting advice.

Finally, if you are doing battle with some authority or other over some grave injustice and you have failed to get anywhere with a direct approach or through an association or federation, don't forget the Ombudsman.

Customer Relations

Let us move on and look at some other types of public relations. Customer relations is partly PR and partly simple business sense, but it is an important factor in the crucial difference between success and failure.

If people are made to feel wanted they will come again . . . and again. But if your staff are surly, the premises dirty or the beer flat, only a handful of customers will actually complain. Most just won't bother to come back.

Always put yourself in the customer's shoes. Take a look at the shop at regular intervals to see what sort of welcome people are given. When out on business, phone the office occasionally to see what response you get from the telephonist, bearing in mind that the person answering the telephone is often a customer's first point of contact with the company.

That receptionist may give *you* a cheerful welcome when you arrive in the morning, but what sort of reception do the *visitors* get? If you don't know, isn't it time you found out? How often do you talk to your staff about how they handle customers? Many successful High Street stores do it once a week.

There are many ways of keeping the customers satisfied, including newsletters and 'open houses'. Quite a few companies open their doors to the clients every so often for a drinks party. It can be combined with a sales promotion (the launch of a new car at a dealer showroom, for example) or simply held once a year to make people feel wanted. The cost of laying on some cheap plonk and a few canapés will be repaid many times over in customer loyalty

Employees

The best PR people of all are your own staff. An employee who really believes in the company can sell it 24 hours a day. Say you employ 10 people. Over the course of a year each might talk in glowing terms about the firm to 100 others. If they in turn are impressed enough to mention it to, let us say, another 50 contacts, the word can get around to 50,000 people who end up with the impression that you make good products, know what you are doing and are good to work for.

To achieve this the staff need to feel involved in the company. The incredible success of the Japanese, for example, stems largely from the family spirit of their industry. Each employee, however menial his or her task, has a sense of responsibility to the corporate entity.

In a small company this sense of belonging can be achieved fairly easily, though not many firms do so. The accountant tends to beaver away at the figures behind closed doors while the salesman is out on the road all day, the managing director is locked in his office and the people at the counter — crucial to PR — never see anyone but irate customers.

The larger the company, the greater is the need for a communication network, with a disciplined passing on of information about the company. If the head of the firm or department gets together with the dozen or so people below him or her once a month in company time, he or she can brief them on progress, products, policies and anything else which can help them to know *why* they are doing *what* they are doing.

At the same time the employees can raise any questions or points of their own, which in turn can be an eye-opener to the boss, who had not realised that the warehouse was too cold or that several customers had said they would buy twice as much tonic wine if it were three pence a bottle cheaper.

Above all, involve your staff in your PR activities. Every so often a group of you can have a brainstorming session for PR ideas, perhaps with a prize for anyone whose idea is put into practice. Or get them to do some basic research for you by going out with a clipboard and getting opinions or reactions from the public to your product or service.

Job Advertisements

PR benefits can come out of a whole range of employee activities. Even a simple job advertisement can be used to help the company's public image. Instead of simply advertising for a new warehouse hand or chairman, use the space to describe what a great company it is to work for and what a good crowd the other employees are. Don't forget that job advertisements are seen by thousands of people, not just the prospective candidates.

Bringing People on to the Premises

While the principle of 'open houses' for existing clients can apply to any type of company, many firms will gain by luring members of the general public on to the premises. DIY stores, garden centres, shops and a host of others can boost sales by increasing the number of people who come through the door.

A good example of how to attract potential customers at very little cost was the manufacturer of simulated fur coats who advertised in a Women's Institute handbook. He invited members to organise visits to the factory to see how imitation fur coats were made.

It made an attractive deal for the WIs, which are always on the look-out for interesting activities. And what could be nearer their hearts than a fur coat company! All they had to do was ring up to arrange the date, announce it to the members and hire the coach.

For the company it was a great promotional idea. The cost was just one small ad in the handbook plus the time of someone to show the ladies round the factory. Yet it was right on target, aiming at the very group of people most likely to want to buy the product and getting them on to the premises to feast their eyes on all those lovely fur coats.

Similarly, a car dealer held a local children's art competition. In addition to the prizes there was a guarantee that all the entries would be displayed in the showrooms for a week. It was held in school holiday time and gave the youngsters something to do. The benefit for the car dealer was that all those little budding Picassos dragged Mum and Dad along to the showroom to proudly show them their efforts hanging on a display board. Once there, they found the cars infinitely more interesting than the paintings . . .

Will this sort of idea work for your business? Not too good for, say, an office service, but how about a dress shop organising a 'modelling school' with free lessons from an expert? Local young hopefuls can try their hand at modelling — free. All they have to do is come to the shop. Or a shoemaker could invite PTAs to come and see how the best children's shoes are made. And so on.

It is more than just an 'open house'. It's a case of asking yourself:

☐ Who is most likely to buy my product?
☐ What will attract them most about a visit to my premises?
☐ How do I get to them?

Seminars and Forums

Depending on your line of business, organising some kind of seminar or forum can be an inspired piece of public relations. People love going to courses, seminars, conferences, and any other activities which give them a chance to (1) get away from the office (on expenses), (2) meet other people in the same line of business, (3) have a good time away from home, and, optionally, (4) learn something.

Examples might include:

1. A supplier of audio visual equipment who organises a practical seminar on 'Audio visual communication for businessmen'.
2. A publisher who runs a one-day course to discuss copyright procedure for journalists, authors etc.
3. A safety equipment company which holds a seminar on 'How to make your business safe'.
4. The local branch of a representative body which holds a regional conference on two-tier boards, or entitled 'What the new Finance Act means', or on whatever happens to be the problem of the day.

Often these occasions are organised under the auspices of a body which sounds authoritative. The communication seminar might be co-sponsored by the Institute of Something-or-Other (there probably is one) while the business conference could be held at the nearby university and chaired by the Professor of Business Studies.

This is because organising a seminar gives you an air of authority on a subject. In the public mind you are not flogging your wares but standing aloof from commercial interests to give the benefit of your academic wisdom to others. The involvement of a professional or educational body enhances this impression of credibility still further.

It hardly matters that you don't know the first thing about the safety of buildings or the law of copyright, because you are going to hire genuine experts to give the talks and answer questions anyway. Your part in it is to get the company's name associated in the public mind with your field of business. It is very powerful, low-key selling. Even the advertising and leaflets for the course are plugs for your company.

A conference or seminar can be quite expensive to organise. There are speakers' fees, food, accommodation, advertising and mailing of leaflets. But, of course, you will charge the delegates (if it is free it immediately becomes more promotional and less authoritative) so the final expense may be relatively small. You may even make a profit!

On the same principle, though further down the market, you could consider holding forums. For example, a sportswear shop might hold a sports forum, with the boss as chairman and two or three sporting stars on the panel. As well as attracting people to the forum itself, the firm would put out a press release in advance and get the event reported on the night.

Publications and Guides

This is another 'stamp of authority' idea. Say you are an insurance broker. It would not cost much to publish an eight-page guide to the insurance jungle: how to insure your house, the best form of life policy, how to get the most from your savings, what to insure.

If you run a catering company you could prepare a booklet, with checklists, on 'What you need for the wedding'. At the back would be an appropriate reminder that your company can take all the hassle out of ordering the cake and plying the guests with drinks. Prospective recipients might be tracked down from the names of hapless brides' fathers in the announcements columns, and you could give a free supply of the booklet to the local vicars, who are usually the first port of call for would-be married couples.

The idea can be applied to almost anything. Look, for example, at the credibility given to CAMRA (Campaign for Real Ale) by the production of its *Good Beer Guide*. As well as promoting CAMRA and encouraging people to drink real ale, the book has a cover price and is a source of revenue in its own right.

Competitions and Awards

You have seen them in the papers: 'Win a fabulous car'; 'Thousands of super paddling pools to be won'; 'A year's supply of dog food — just put the names to the famous faces'. These competitions are usually joint efforts by a newspaper and a manufacturer to promote sales of both the paper and the company's products. The publicity and the glittering prizes are beneficial to both parties, and of course to the general public who are given a one-in-a-million chance of eating free dog food for a year.

In the national newspapers the prizes are pretty high-powered and can usually only be afforded by the big manufacturers. But local papers are full of competitions for things like a week-end for two in Bournemouth or a free hair-do. It may be that your service or product would make a good prize, in which case it is worth contacting the local paper to see if it is interested in running a competition.

Often the contests involve box-ticking or matching things up. See if there is some way in which you can relate the competition more directly to your product, like the win-a-car competitions where you have to list the car's good points in order of importance.

Don't forget any industrial staff newspaper in the area, and if the newspapers can't play ball you can always consider printing competition leaflets and using a distribution service to put them through letter boxes.

If the competition involves potential customers having to come on to the premises to collect something or fill in a form — and in the process they see your products — then so much the better.

Another publicity tool can be the establishment of an award of some sort. We have looked at some of these ('best student nurse' etc) in Chapter 7, but the principle can be applied more generally. It is the sort of thing that the press likes and it need cost no more than, say, £100 for a trophy, £100 or so as a cash prize, a press/VIP reception to announce the winner (this is not essential if you are operating on a shoestring, but is good extra publicity), and a certain amount of administrative time. Awards can range from the serious ('Widcastle businessman of the year') to the light-hearted ('Friendliest publican in town').

Stunts and Circus Tricks

Although the PR 'profession' frowns on it, there is still plenty of good old-fashioned public relations around. The days of barnstorming and tight-ropes across skyscrapers are not over. People do strange things in balloons, break records for the fastest steamroller and sponsor crazy contests.

The name of the game is grabbing attention. The public, and the press in particular, are always glad of something different, some refreshing stunt which makes you do a double-take or which can attract a few 'oohs' and 'ahs' from a big crowd.

There are those who frown on the use of publicity stunts and disown them as not being a part of PR. However, if something arouses interest in your product or company name, in a beneficial light, then it is surely establishing relations with the public.

As well as getting publicity, a good stunt can also be fun, and there is not enough of that in business. The main things to watch out for are that it doesn't cost too much and that it is not so stupid that it invites criticism or reflects ill upon your company.

There will, of course, be those occasions when the whole thing is a resounding flop — when it pours with rain, no one turns up, someone forgets the gas for the balloon and the press photographer has got the wrong date in his diary. But by and large the occasional circus trick can do you and your business a lot of good. However, there is not much a book can do when it comes to thinking up bright ideas. There is no formula. You just have to cook up your own or pinch somebody else's.

Here, though, are a few case histories of what some business people have done to attract attention in different ways. They might get your mind going in the right direction.

On the first day of the 'season', the first grouse was shot at dawn. There then followed an elaborate trek as the unfortunate creature was rushed by foot, motorbike, helicopter, plane, car, and finally parachute, to a venue in the south of England. Were they rushing it to a specialist hospital for an emergency operation? No, all the fuss and expense were incurred by a restaurant which wanted to serve the first grouse of the season.

Farcical it may have sounded. But the name of the restaurant appeared in all the national newspapers and was mentioned on several national TV and radio broadcasts. The main TV news of the evening filmed the process in detail and gave the restaurant several free plugs.

There was criticism from various quarters, notably the culinary world which was horrified that the grouse hadn't been hung first (and presumably given a fair trial before that), but you can't argue with publicity which would have cost way over £100,000 in advertising costs, and some of which (eg BBC News) could not have been bought anyway.

On a simpler note, there was the local butcher who was confronted one Yuletide by an itinerant artist who had fallen on hard times. The deal was simple: in return for a week's free meat the artist would turn the shop window into a giant pastoral scene full of cows, chickens and other meaty things.

It was such a hit that it is still there. Regular customers told their friends, who went along for a look and ended up becoming customers themselves. It made a story in the local press and featured in the national butchers' magazine. The idea could hardly have been more simple. But it was *different* and that is what counts.

Then there was the famous 'car wars' case in Florida. In fact, this was a highly professional and expensive operation but the idea could be borrowed for other purposes much more cheaply.

It all started when a Chevrolet dealer walked publicly into his local Ford dealership and smashed a 'Ford has a better idea' light bulb.

Incensed, the Ford man flew a helicopter over the Chevrolet showrooms and 'bombed' it with 10,000 ping-pong balls. The 'war' lasted for two long months: effigies were hung on forecourts, live rabbits released in showrooms and a gravestone erected to mark the demise of one or other of the two adversaries. Every new battle in the war brought local and national press flocking to the scene and, more importantly, thousands of spectators would crowd into the dealership whose turn it was to be attacked.

All this aggro had actually started before the first incident, when the two dealers were bemoaning a slack period and hit on a way of getting some joint publicity. Behind the scenes they remained the best of friends and the two sales staffs had regular meetings to engineer the course of the war. Though it had the look of a no holds barred contest, both sides avoided knocking each other's products or integrity. That would have been counter-productive to both of them. And the campaign had a bottom line in the form of 140 more cars sold than usual. That's a lot of publicity-inspired turnover.

There are innumerable ways of organising publicity stunts. One week's reading of the newspapers can produce a range of ideas, such as the apple growers who went and distributed their wares round the offices of Fleet Street, or the butchers who formed a 'Save our sausage society'.

That's one of the lovely things about PR. It is going on around you all the time and the ideas are there for the borrowing. There are no set rules or conventions, and your way of doing it is probably just as good as that of the seasoned pro or expensive consultant.

It is all about making your various publics aware of you, interested in your products or services, and favourable to the way you operate, even if they are not sure how they got that opinion in the first place.

You might spend a lot of money achieving this, or you might equally achieve considerable publicity for free. Often a good idea is better than a great deal of money. Like a high standard of golf, it is something which comes naturally if you keep practising and programming your mind to opportunities and methods.

And what better way to start than to ask yourself: *Why pay to advertise?*

Further Reading from Kogan Page

The Business Guide to Effective Speaking, Jacqueline Dunckel and Elizabeth Parnham, 1985

Getting Sales, Richard D Smith and Ginger Dick, 1984

How to Organize Effective Conferences and Meetings, David Seekings, Third edition 1987

Practical Sponsorship, Stuart Turner, 1987

Promoting Yourself on Television and Radio, Michael Bland, 1987

Promotion for the Profesisons, Ian Linton, 1985

PR Week Marketing and Public Relations Handbook 1987, ed Geoffrey Lace